Company's Coming

diabetic
cooking

*Great tasting recipes
for the entire family*

Diabetic Cooking

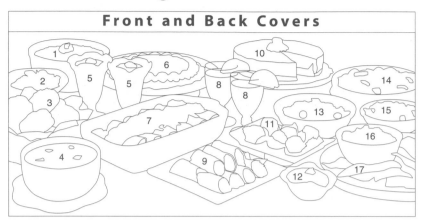

Front and Back Covers

Diabetic Cooking
Copyright © Company's Coming
         Publishing Limited
All rights reserved worldwide. No part of this book may be reproduced in any form by any means without written permission in advance from the publisher. Brief portions of this book may be reproduced for review purposes, provided credit is given to the source. Reviewers are invited to contact the publisher for additional information.

Second printing March 2001

Canadian Cataloguing in
Publication Data
Main entry under title:
  Diabetic cooking
Issued also in French under title:
  La cuisine diabétique
Includes indexes.
  ISBN 1893455-49-9
  1. Diabetes–Diet therapy–Recipes. 2. Diabetes–Nutritional aspects.

R662.D52 2001   641.5'6314   C00-901276-1

Published simultaneously in
Canada and the United States of America
by Company's Coming
Publishing Limited
2311 - 96 Street
Edmonton, Alberta, Canada
T6N 1G3
Tel: 780 • 450-6223
Fax: 780 • 450-1857
www.companyscoming.com

Our special thanks to the following businesses for providing extensive props for photography.
The Bay
Winners

Diabetic Cooking is produced in cooperation with

Juvenile Diabetes Foundation Canada
The Diabetes Research Foundation

For further information
please contact:
www.jdfc.ca or **1-877-CURE JDF**

COOKBOOKS

Company's Coming is a registered trademark owned by Company's Coming Publishing Limited

Cooking Tonight?
Drop by companyscoming.com

companyscoming.com

| Who We Are | Browse Cookbooks | Cooking Tonight? | Home |

everyday ingredients

feature recipes

- feature recipes
- tips and tricks
- table talk
- cooking links
- experts on-line
- keyword search

- e-mail us

Company's Coming
COOKBOOKS®

everyday
recipes trusted
by millions

Cooking tonight? Check out this month's *feature recipes*—absolutely FREE!

Looking for some great kitchen helpers? *tips and tricks* is here to save the day!

In search of answers to cooking or household questions? Do you have answers you'd like to share? Join the fun with *table talk*, our on-line question and answer bulletin board. Our *table talk chat room* connects you with cooks from around the world. Great for swapping recipes too!

Other interesting and informative web-sites are just a click away with *cooking links*.

Consult *experts on-line* for Jean Paré's time-saving tips and advice.

Find cookbooks by title, description or food category using *keyword search*.

We want to hear from you—*e-mail us* lets you offer suggestions for upcoming titles, or share your favorite recipes.

Company's Coming
cookbooks

ORIGINAL SERIES		
	150 Delicious Squares	Low-Fat Pasta
	Appliance Cooking **NEW**	Make-Ahead Meals
	(April 1/01)	Main Courses
	Appetizers	Meatless Cooking
	Barbecues	Muffins & More
	Breads	One-Dish Meals
	Breakfasts & Brunches	Pasta
	Cakes	Pies
	Casseroles	Pizza!
	Chicken, Etc.	Preserves
	Cookies	Salads
	Cooking for Two	Soups & Sandwiches
	Desserts	Slow Cooker Recipes
	Kids Cooking	Starters
	Light Casseroles	Stir-Fry
	Light Recipes	The Potato Book
	Low-Fat Cooking	Vegetables

LIFESTYLE SERIES	
	Diabetic Cooking **NEW**
	Grilling
	Low-fat Cooking
	Low-fat Pasta

GREATEST HITS	
	Biscuits, Muffins & Loaves
	Dips, Spreads & Dressings
	Italian **NEW** (May 1/01)
	Mexican **NEW** (May 1/01)
	Sandwiches & Wraps
	Soups & Salads

SPECIAL OCCASION SERIES	
	Chocolate Everything

Table of contents

The Company's Coming

story

Jean Paré grew up understanding that the combination of family, friends and home cooking is the essence of a good life. From her mother she learned to appreciate good cooking, while her father praised even her earliest attempts. When she left home she took with her many acquired family recipes, a love of cooking and an intriguing desire to read recipe books like novels!

"never share a recipe you wouldn't use yourself"

In 1963, when her four children had all reached school age, Jean volunteered to cater the 50th anniversary of the Vermilion School of Agriculture, now Lakeland College. Working out of her home, Jean prepared a dinner for over 1000 people which launched a flourishing catering operation that continued for over eighteen years. During that time she was provided with countless opportunities to test new ideas with immediate feedback—resulting in empty plates and contented customers! Whether preparing cocktail sandwiches for a house party or serving a hot meal for 1500 people, Jean Paré earned a reputation for good food, courteous service and reasonable prices.

"Why don't you write a cookbook?" Time and again, as requests for her recipes mounted, Jean was asked that question. Jean's response was to team up with her son, Grant Lovig, in the fall of 1980 to form Company's Coming Publishing Limited. April 14, 1981, marked the debut of "150 DELICIOUS SQUARES", the first Company's Coming cookbook in what soon would become Canada's most popular cookbook series.

Jean Paré's operation has grown steadily from the early days of working out of a spare bedroom in her home. Full-time staff includes marketing personnel located in major cities across Canada. Home Office is based in Edmonton, Alberta in a modern building constructed specially for the company.

Today the company distributes throughout Canada and the United States in addition to numerous overseas markets, all under the guidance of Jean's daughter, Gail Lovig. Best-sellers many times over, Company's Coming cookbooks are published in English and French, plus a Spanish-language edition is available in Mexico. Familiar and trusted in home kitchens the world over, Company's Coming cookbooks are offered in a variety of formats, including the original softcover series.

Jean Paré's approach to cooking has always called for quick and easy recipes using everyday ingredients. Even when traveling, she is constantly on the lookout for new ideas to share with her readers. At home, she can usually be found researching and writing recipes, or working in the company's test kitchen.

Jean continues to gain new supporters by adhering to what she calls "the golden rule of cooking": never share a recipe you wouldn't use yourself. It's an approach that works—*millions of times over!*

foreword

When a family member has diabetes, all too often it has meant cooking one meal for him or her, and cooking a different meal for the rest of the family. No longer. Now the entire family can enjoy tasty recipes and benefit from a well-balanced eating plan with *Diabetic Cooking*. What could be better? Treat your family to great-tasting, kitchen-tested recipes that have the added perks of being low in fat and sugar.

Over the years many of my readers have asked for a diabetic cookbook, so I had thought of creating one well before my husband Larry was diagnosed with Type 2 diabetes. With today's focus on healthy eating, I admit to baking less, if only to provide fewer temptations around the house.

Many people with diabetes miss their desserts, but they can fit treats into their daily meals in consultation with a dietitian. Check out the Desserts section for Strawberry Banana Frozen Yogurt, French Pastry Dessert or Lemon Angel Tower.

From the first page to the last, *Diabetic Cooking* is designed to bring you great-tasting food. Try Crispy Barbecue Chips with Black Bean And Corn

Salsa as a snack or appetizer for a party, or whip up some Honey Wheat Bread for lunch with Couscous Seafood Salad. Fix Jambalaya Casserole or quick and easy Creamy Garlic Penne for supper. How about Special Plum Chicken with a side dish of Cheese Spirals or Stuffed Tomatoes? When you feel like celebrating a special occasion, concoct a batch of out-of-this-world Brownies or Cherry Chocolate Dessert. Share them and be prepared for rave reviews from all!

During development of this book, we convened a focus group of people of all ages with diabetes to sample our recipes. They held us up to their high standards, making sure this book would meet with your approval too. After all, food that's good for you needs to taste good enough to eat!

We also wish to thank the dedicated volunteers and staff of the Juvenile Diabetes Foundation for their valued input and encouragement.

Whether you have diabetes, are cooking for someone who has diabetes, or are just interested in a healthier lifestyle, you'll be glad you picked up your copy of *Diabetic Cooking!*

Jean Paré

each recipe

has been analyzed using the most updated version of the Canadian Nutrient File from Health and Welfare Canada, which is based upon the United States Department of Agriculture (USDA) Nutrient Data Base.

Margaret Ng, B.Sc. (Hon), M.A.
Registered Dietitian

About Diabetes

When someone has diabetes, their blood has too much glucose — a type of sugar — because their body isn't processing it properly. The body receives glucose from digestion of carbohydrates such as those found in grains, fruits and vegetables, and milk. The liver also produces glucose that travels into the blood stream.

Under healthy conditions, the pancreas produces enough insulin to enable glucose to enter cells and be used as fuel. People with Type 1 (or insulin-dependent) diabetes have a severe lack of insulin because their pancreas produces little or none at all. In order to maintain normal blood glucose levels, they need to take insulin injections and control their intake of fats and carbohydrates.

People with Type 2 (or non insulin-dependent) diabetes still produce insulin, but not enough, or their body does not use it efficiently. They may be able to manage their disease with diet alone or with a combination of diet and pills and/or insulin injections.

Without treatment, symptoms of diabetes may include increased thirst and urination, fatigue, vision changes and weight loss. In the long term, diabetes can damage the eyes, kidneys, nerves, heart and circulation system. Being physically active and maintaining a healthy body weight are keys to good living for everyone, but critical for those with diabetes.

Diabetic Cooking is a cookbook filled with enticing, easy-to-prepare food. It follows the theory that dietary guidelines for people with diabetes are the same for everyone: eat a wide variety of nutritious food in moderation. Every person with diabetes needs to consult with a dietitian to determine his or her personal eating plan.

No foods are forbidden — limiting alcohol consumption, salt, fat and sugar doesn't necessarily mean *eliminating* those items. Just like putting the wrong kind of gasoline in your car affects performance, fueling your body with poor food choices does the same thing. The cost of eating "premium fuel," doesn't have to be a premium price. Some cuts of meat may seem pricey, but not when you consider a portion of steak as 4 oz. (113 g), rather than 8 oz. (225 g). Likewise, fresh fruits and vegetables fluctuate in price, so buy fruit in season and then compare cost to its processed cousin-in-a-can. Convenience foods are often high in fat, salt and sugar, so stay clear of them, and keep only your wallet fatter!

Advice about sugar consumption for people with diabetes has changed over the years. Small quantities of sugar that don't cause a quick peak in blood sugar levels are now allowed. A large soft drink or chocolate bar will have a lot of concentrated sugar, but a small piece of chocolate or candy will have a lesser effect on blood glucose levels.

Fresh fruit and ice cream are simple desserts or snacks and, in small quantities, have lower fat than regular cheese and crackers. Foods like nuts, salami and olives are also high in fat, so low-fat cheese, dips and breads would be preferable as fill-ins between meals. If you can, find yummy add-ons like a wonderful low-fat salad dressing from our Sauces section to go with "free" foods (those without quantity restrictions), such as green and leafy vegetables or salad vegetables!

While starchy foods may cause blood sugar spikes, they are still carbohydrates, which is something every body needs. Complex carbohydrates with fiber (generally foods which have not been highly processed) are more nutritious and better at keeping blood glucose levels on an even keel.

Diabetic Choices (Exchanges)

Once a person has been diagnosed with diabetes, he or she needs to meet with a dietitian who will work out a plan outlining the types and amounts of foods they can eat for each snack and meal. Similar foods are grouped together in categories as fruits & vegetables, protein foods (meat and meat substitutes), milk, fat & oil, and starch/bread. One choice (exchange) in each category varies in size but all have about the same composition of carbohydrates, protein, fat and calories. Once people with diabetes know how many and what kinds of choices (exchanges) they need to eat daily, it's mostly a matter of keeping track to keep blood glucose levels stable. We have included diabetic choices (exchanges) to make it easy for you to fit these recipes into your daily life.

Nutrition Information

For each recipe in *Diabetic Cooking*, we have provided nutrition information, which tallies calories, fat (including cholesterol and saturated fats), carbohydrate, protein and sodium. These values include all the ingredients listed in the recipe except those, which are stated as optional, or garnishes. If a range of measurements is given, the first amount is analyzed. Variations of recipes are listed underneath the analysis and are not included.

The Recipes in this Cookbook

◆ **Artificial Sweeteners:** When testing the recipes in *Diabetic Cooking*, we did not use artificial with the exception of a few recipes where a large amount of sugar would have been required or because we wanted to provide some recipes where a substitute would work.

◆ **Fats:** We chose to use canola or olive oil instead of margarine where we could. In some recipes, margarine or butter was better for taste, but we limited the amount. Butter can be used moderately, but it is an animal fat and contains cholesterol. All fat and oils contain 9 calories per gram (compared to 4 calories per gram for carbohydrates), but vegetable or olive oil is better for your arteries. Where possible, we used non-stick cookware or no-stick cooking spray to reduce the fats and oils used.

◆ **Meats:** All the meat we used was trimmed of fat prior to cooking. We also chose lean cuts of meat such as boneless, skinless chicken breasts or beef sirloin.

◆ **Milk:** Our test kitchen staff used skim milk unless specified, since it has an equal amount of calcium and approximately the same amount of nutrients as 1%, 2% or whole milk, without any of the animal fat.

◆ **Egg Substitute:** Most of our recipes call for only one or two eggs. In the cases where we have used egg substitute, it was because more than two eggs were needed or was considered an "egg" dish. Sometimes we chose an egg substitute because the recipe already had other saturated fats. You may also choose to buy "designer eggs," for healthier reasons. If preferred, avoid egg yolks from eggs, to reduce fat and cholesterol; the whites contain high quality protein without the fat.

◆ **Cheese:** We used light sharp Cheddar cheese or part-skim mozzarella or grated light Parmesan cheese product to lower the fat content without compromising taste.

◆ **Yogurt:** These recipes were tested using plain and flavored non-fat yogurt. With a little imagination and minimal effort, you can make Yogurt Cheese, page 75, as a creamy substitute for cream cheese.

◆ **Cooking Methods:** We recommend baking, grilling, steaming, poaching and stir-frying to reduce the amount of fat needed to cook an item and keep more of the nutrients.

If you have any questions about how these recipes, or any other food, can fit into the diet of someone with diabetes, please talk to your doctor or dietitian.

Boosters

Boosters are high-sugar snacks designed to jumpstart your sugar levels when they plummet, so don't substitute the sugar-free version of flavored gelatin. However, using the lower-fat products is a good idea. These boosters are meant to be frozen in individual portions and taken along with you for emergencies.

Take-Along Treat

Container of vanilla frosting	16 oz.	450 g
Almond flavoring	¼ tsp.	1 mL
White corn syrup	⅓ cup	75 mL
Finely chopped dried apricots	1½ cups	375 mL
Icing (confectioner's) sugar	3 cups	750 mL
Flake coconut	1 cup	250 mL
Icing (confectioner's) sugar (optional)		
Flake coconut (optional)		

Combine frosting and flavoring in large bowl.

Measure corn syrup into small bowl. Microwave on high (100%) for 30 seconds or warm in small saucepan on low. Stir in apricots until well coated. Add to frosting. Stir well.

Stir in icing sugar and coconut. Knead with hands to combine well. Turn out onto flat surface. Knead, adding icing sugar if required to prevent sticking, until smooth. Measure into ½ tbsp. (7 mL) portions. Roll into balls.

Roll in additional icing sugar or coconut. Wrap individual balls in plastic wrap. Freeze. Makes about 52 balls.

NUTRITION INFORMATION 1 ball: 85 Calories; 1.1 g Total Fat (0.7 g Sat., 1.7 mg Cholesterol); 10 mg Sodium; trace Protein; 20 g Carbohydrate; trace Dietary Fiber

CHOICES 1 Fruit & Vegetable; 1 Sugar

Sweet Cereal Chews

Light smooth peanut butter	½ cup	125 mL
Corn syrup	¼ cup	60 mL
Miniature marshmallows	3 cups	750 mL
Vanilla	½ tsp.	2 mL
Corn flakes cereal	5 cups	1.25 L

Melt peanut butter and corn syrup in large saucepan on low. Stir in marshmallows until just melted. Do not overcook. Remove from heat.

Stir in vanilla and cereal until well coated. Press firmly into greased 9 x 9 inch (22 x 22 cm) pan. Cool to room temperature. Cut into 24 bars. Wrap individual bars in plastic wrap. Freeze. Makes 24 bars.

NUTRITION INFORMATION 1 bar: 84 Calories; 2.3 g Total Fat (0.4 g Sat., 0.01 mg Cholesterol); 96 mg Sodium; 2 g Protein; 15 g Carbohydrate; trace Dietary Fiber

CHOICES 1 Sugar

Loopy O's Treat

Margarine	2 tbsp.	30 mL
White corn syrup	⅓ cup	75 mL
Package of fruit-flavored gelatin (jelly powder), your favorite (not sugar-free)	3 oz.	85 g
"O"-shaped fruity cereal (such as Fruit Loops)	4 cups	1 L

Melt margarine in large saucepan on medium. Stir in corn syrup and jelly powder. Heat and stir until boiling and jelly powder is dissolved. Remove from heat.

Quickly stir in cereal to coat. Mixture is very sticky, so work fast. Press firmly into greased foil-lined 8 x 8 inch (20 x 20 cm) square pan. Chill just until set. Cut into 18 bars. Wrap individual bars in plastic wrap. Freeze. Makes 18 bars.

NUTRITION INFORMATION 1 bar: 74 Calories; 1.4 g Total Fat (0.3 g Sat., 0 mg Cholesterol); 60 mg Sodium; 1 g Protein; 15 g Carbohydrate; trace Dietary Fiber

CHOICES ½ Fruit & Vegetable; 1 Sugar

Appetizers & Beverages

Whether you want an appetite teaser or a thirst quencher, the recipes in this section provide a tasty touch to an ordinary eating experience! These dips and sauces can liven up a variety of main courses, or they can be served with crackers or breads for company. Sip the drinks slowly to savor each delicious mouthful.

Stuffed Grapevine Leaves

The fragrance while they're baking will make you very impatient to taste them! These work well served warm as a finger food-appetizer. Serve with Fresh Yogurt Sauce, page 13.

Chopped onion	1 cup	250 mL
Garlic cloves, minced	2	2
Olive oil	2 tsp.	10 mL
Brown rice	1⅓ cups	325 mL
Medium tomato, chopped	1	1
Water	2¾ cups	675 mL
Chicken bouillon powder	1 tsp.	5 mL
Freshly ground pepper, sprinkle		
Chopped fresh parsley	2 tbsp.	30 mL
Raisins, chopped	¼ cup	60 mL
Pine nuts, toasted and chopped	¼ cup	60 mL
Ground cinnamon	¼ tsp.	1 mL
Jar of grapevine leaves, drained	17 oz.	473 mL
Water	½ cup	125 mL
Olive oil	1 tbsp.	15 mL
Lemon juice	2 tbsp.	30 mL

Sauté onion and garlic in olive oil in large non-stick frying pan until onion is soft. Add rice. Cook until rice is toasted. Turn into large saucepan.

Stir in next 8 ingredients. Bring to a boil. Cover. Cook for about 40 minutes until rice is tender. Makes 4½ cups (1.1 L).

Prepare vine leaves by pinching off any stem ends. Using larger leaves, place about 2 rounded tablespoons (30 mL) filling on underside of leaf, near stem end. Roll up, tucking in sides to enclose filling. Repeat until rice mixture is used up. Use any leftover vine leaves to line greased 3 quart (3 L) casserole. Place rolls seam side down and very close to each other in 2 layers.

Combine water, olive oil and lemon juice in small cup. Drizzle over rolls. Cover tightly. Bake in 325°F (160°C) oven for 1½ hours until leaves are very tender and all liquid is absorbed. Makes 28 appetizers.

NUTRITION INFORMATION 1 appetizer: 60 Calories; 2 g Total Fat (0.3 g Sat., trace Cholesterol); 76 mg Sodium; 2 g Protein; 10 g Carbohydrate; 1 g Dietary Fiber

CHOICES ½ Starch; ½ Fruit & Vegetable; ½ Fat & Oil

Pictured on page 18.

Fresh Yogurt Sauce

Substitute Yogurt Cheese, page 75, for the yogurt and texture will be thicker — great for a dip or to serve on baked potatoes.

Grated English cucumber, with peel	½ **cup**	**125 mL**
Salt	¼ **tsp.**	**1 mL**
Low-fat plain yogurt	**1 cup**	**250 mL**
Garlic clove, minced	**1**	**1**
Chopped fresh mint leaves (or parsley)	**2 tbsp.**	**30 mL**

Combine cucumber and salt in small bowl. Let stand for 10 minutes. Pour into sieve. Squeeze cucumber until most of liquid is gone. Return to bowl.

Add remaining 3 ingredients. Stir gently. Cover. Chill for 1 hour to blend flavors. Makes 1½ cups (375 mL).

NUTRITION INFORMATION 1 tbsp. (15 mL): 7 Calories; 0.2 g Total Fat (0.1 g Sat., 0.7 mg Cholesterol); 35 mg Sodium; 1 g Protein; 1 g Carbohydrate; trace Dietary Fiber

CHOICES Extra

Pictured on page 18.

Hummus

Serve spread on torn fresh pita or as a thick dip for vegetables.

Garlic cloves	**2**	**2**
Toasted sesame seeds	**4 tbsp.**	**60 mL**
Ground cumin	¼ **tsp.**	**1 mL**
Lemon pepper	¼ **tsp.**	**1 mL**
Lemon juice	**2 tbsp.**	**30 mL**
Can of chick peas (garbanzo beans), drained and liquid reserved	**19 oz.**	**540 mL**
Reserved chick pea liquid, approximately	**7 tbsp.**	**115 mL**

Process garlic cloves, 3 tbsp. (50 mL) sesame seeds, cumin and lemon pepper in blender on high until garlic and sesame seeds are smooth. Add enough lemon juice to make thick paste.

Add chick peas and 3 tbsp. (50 mL) chick pea liquid. Blend with pulsing motion, scraping down sides as necessary, until mixture is puréed. Add approximately 4 tbsp. (60 mL) liquid from chick peas to thin dip to desired consistency. Turn into serving bowl. Sprinkle remaining 1 tbsp. (15 mL) sesame seeds on top. Makes 2 cups (500 mL).

NUTRITION INFORMATION 2 tbsp. (30 mL): 54 Calories; 1.5 g Total Fat (0.1 g Sat., 0 mg Cholesterol); 99 mg Sodium; 2 g Protein; 8 g Carbohydrate; 2 g Dietary Fiber

CHOICES ½ Starch

Salad Rolls

These are so good. Keep for up to two hours in refrigerator under a damp paper towel and wrapped in plastic.

Water	¹/₃ cup	75 mL
Thick teriyaki sauce	2 tbsp.	30 mL
Low-sodium soy sauce	1 tbsp.	15 mL
Cornstarch	2 tsp.	10 mL
Fish sauce (optional), see Note	¹/₄-¹/₂ tsp.	1-2 mL
Shredded lettuce, lightly packed	2 cups	500 mL
Chopped fresh bean sprouts	1 cup	250 mL
Green onion, thinly sliced	1	1
Fresh sweet basil leaves, cut chiffonade (see Tip, page 15)	12	12
Fresh pea pods, chopped (optional)	¹/₃ cup	75 mL
Grated carrot	¹/₃ cup	75 mL
Chopped imitation crabmeat (or shrimp)	³/₄ cup	175 mL
Rice vermicelli	1 oz.	28 g
Hot water		
Rice paper wrappers (8 inch, 20 cm, size)	12	12
Warm water		
PEANUT SAUCE		
Light smooth peanut butter	¹/₂ cup	125 mL
Plain skim milk yogurt	¹/₂ cup	125 mL
Medium-hot curry paste (see Note)	1 ¹/₂ tsp.	7 mL
Chili paste (optional)	¹/₄ tsp.	1 mL
Lime juice	1 ¹/₂ tsp.	7 mL
Finely chopped peanuts, for garnish		

Combine first 5 ingredients in small saucepan. Heat and stir on medium until boiling and thickened. Cool thoroughly.

Combine lettuce, bean sprouts, onion, basil, pea pods, carrot and crab in medium bowl. Set aside.

Break vermicelli into small pieces in small bowl. Cover with hot water. Let stand for 3 minutes until softened. Drain. Rinse with cold water. Drain thoroughly. Add to lettuce mixture. Toss.

(continued on next page)

Soak each rice wrapper in warm water in 9 inch (22 cm) pie plate for 2 minutes until soft. Place packed ⅓ cup (75 mL) lettuce mixture across one side of center, leaving 1 inch (2.5 cm) piece of wrapper on each side uncovered. Drizzle 2 tsp. (10 mL) sauce over filling. Fold sides of wrapper over filling. Roll tightly over filling. Press gently at seam to seal. Place on serving platter. Cover with damp paper towel to keep from drying out. Repeat with remaining wrappers and filling. Cut each roll in half crosswise to serve. Makes 12 rolls or 24 half rolls.

Peanut Sauce: Whisk all 6 ingredients together in small bowl until smooth. Let stand at room temperature for 10 minutes to blend flavors. Makes 1 cup (250 mL) sauce.

NUTRITION INFORMATION 1 full roll with 2 tsp. (10 mL) sauce: 82 Calories; 2.5 g Total Fat (0.4 g Sat., 3.5 mg Cholesterol); 237 mg Sodium; 3 g Protein; 11 g Carbohydrate; trace Dietary Fiber

CHOICES ½ Starch; ½ Fruit & Vegetable; ½ Milk; ½ Fat & Oil

Pictured on front cover, on page 18 and on back cover.

Note: Both fish sauce and curry paste are available in Asian section of grocery store.

Herb Dip

Good with any cut-up vegetables. The flavor is much better when made a day ahead.

Plain skim milk yogurt	1 cup	250 mL
Fat-free salad dressing	¼ cup	60 mL
Parsley flakes	2 tsp.	10 mL
Chopped fresh chives (or 2 tsp., 10 mL, dried)	1 tbsp.	15 mL
Dried whole oregano, crushed	½ tsp.	2 mL
Dried sweet basil	½ tsp.	2 mL
Dried tarragon leaves, crushed	⅛-¼ tsp.	0.5-1 mL
Dry mustard	1 tsp.	5 mL
Salt	½ tsp.	2 mL
Granulated sugar	½ tsp.	2 mL

Combine all 10 ingredients in small bowl. Cover. Chill for at least two hours to blend flavors. Makes 1⅛ cups (280 mL).

NUTRITION INFORMATION 1 tbsp. (15 mL): 12 Calories; 0.1 g Total Fat (trace Sat., 0.3 mg Cholesterol); 110 mg Sodium; 1 g Protein; 2 g Carbohydrate; trace Dietary Fiber

CHOICES Extra

To cut basil chiffonade: stack leaves, roll tightly lengthwise and then thinly slice crosswise.

Crab Appetizers

These little morsels are good hot or cold. Serve with seafood dipping sauce.

Finely chopped imitation crabmeat	**2 cups**	**500 mL**
Fine dry bread crumbs	**¾ cup**	**175 mL**
Creamed horseradish	**1 tsp.**	**5 mL**
Chopped green onion	**½ cup**	**125 mL**
Finely chopped red or yellow pepper	**½ cup**	**125 mL**
Chopped fresh parsley (or 1 tsp., 5 mL, flakes)	**1 tbsp.**	**15 mL**
Dry mustard	**1 tsp.**	**5 mL**
Salt	**½ tsp.**	**2 mL**
Freshly ground pepper, sprinkle		
Dried sweet basil, crushed	**¼ tsp.**	**1 mL**
Dried whole oregano, crushed	**⅛ tsp.**	**0.5 mL**
Garlic powder (optional)	**⅛ tsp.**	**0.5 mL**
Frozen egg product, thawed (see Note)	**½ cup**	**125 mL**

Combine first 12 ingredients in large bowl. Stir well.

Stir in egg product. Cover with plastic wrap. Chill for 1 hour for crumbs to moisten. Squeeze rounded tablespoonfuls (15 mL) mixture into thirty-four 1½ inch (3.8 cm) balls in palm of hand. Arrange on greased baking sheet. Bake in 350°F (175°C) oven for 10 minutes until firm and golden brown. Makes 34 balls.

NUTRITION INFORMATION 2 balls: 51 Calories; 0.7 g Total Fat (0.1 g Sat., 4.2 mg Cholesterol); 296 mg Sodium; 5 g Protein; 7 g Carbohydrate; trace Dietary Fiber

CHOICES ½ Starch; ½ Protein

Pictured on page 18.

Note: 4 tbsp. (50 mL) =1 large egg

1. Crispy Barbecue Chips, page 21
2. Fresh Tomato Salsa, page 23
3. Piña Colada Smoothie, page 24
4. Black Bean And Corn Salsa, page 21
5. Spicy Mexi-Bean Dip, page 23

Hawaiian Meatballs In Sauce

Serve these with picks for easy handling.

MEATBALLS

Lean ground chicken (or turkey)	1 lb.	454 g
Fine dry bread crumbs	²/₃ cup	150 mL
Large egg	1	1
Prepared mustard	2 tsp.	10 mL
Garlic clove, minced	1	1
Ground ginger	½ tsp.	2 mL
Seasoned salt	½ tsp.	2 mL
Granulated sugar	½ tsp.	2 mL
Finely chopped green onion	¼ cup	60 mL
Can of crushed pineapple, with juice	14 oz.	398 mL

SAUCE

Chili sauce	3 tbsp.	50 mL
Low-sodium soy sauce	2 tbsp.	30 mL
Brown sugar, packed (or sugar substitute)	2 tbsp.	30 mL
Cornstarch	1 tbsp.	15 mL
Water	¼ cup	60 mL

Meatballs: Combine first 9 ingredients with ¼ cup (60 mL) undrained pineapple until mixed well and evenly moist. Reserve remaining pineapple and juice. Form chicken mixture into forty 1 inch (2.5 cm) balls. Place on greased baking sheet. Bake in 400°F (205°C) oven for 12 minutes until meatballs are no longer pink inside. Makes 40 meatballs.

Sauce: Combine chili sauce, soy sauce, brown sugar, cornstarch, water and remaining pineapple with juice in small saucepan. Heat and stir on medium until boiling and slightly thickened. Combine with meatballs. Makes 1⅓ cups (325 mL) sauce.

NUTRITION INFORMATION 1 meatball with ½ tbsp. (7 mL) sauce: 34 Calories; 0.4 g Total Fat (0.1 g Sat., 12 mg Cholesterol); 114 mg Sodium; 3 g Protein; 4 g Carbohydrate; trace Dietary Fiber

CHOICES ½ Fruit & Vegetable; ½ Protein

1. Stuffed Grapevine Leaves, page 12
2. Sushi Layers, page 22
3. Salad Rolls, page 14
4. Crab Appetizers, page 16
5. Fresh Yogurt Sauce, page 13
6. Peanut Sauce, page 14

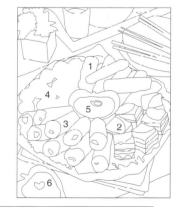

Simple Tuna Spread

Serve with a variety of lower fat crackers. Or take for lunch along with crackers, bread or fresh vegetables. For more flavor, add a little more teriyaki sauce.

Finely chopped red onion	**2 tbsp.**	**30 mL**
Can of white tuna, packed in water, drained and broken into chunks	**6¹/₂ oz.**	**184 g**
Teriyaki sauce	**4-6 tsp.**	**20-30 mL**

Combine onion, tuna and teriyaki sauce in small bowl. Chill for 1 to 2 hours to blend flavors. Makes 1 cup (250 mL).

NUTRITION INFORMATION 1 tbsp. (15 mL): 15 Calories; 0.3 g Total Fat (0.1 g Sat., 4.3 mg Cholesterol); 64 mg Sodium; 3 g Protein; trace Carbohydrate; trace Dietary Fiber

CHOICES ¹/₂ Protein

Variation: Omit teriyaki sauce and add 2 tbsp. (30 mL) non-fat herb and garlic-flavored cream cheese and 2 tsp. (10 mL) low-sodium soy sauce.

Smoked Salmon Mousse

Spread on stoned wheat crackers or baguette slices.

Tomato juice	**¹/₂ cup**	**125 mL**
Envelope of unflavored gelatin	**¹/₄ oz.**	**7 g**
Can of red salmon, drained, skin and round bones removed	**7¹/₂ oz.**	**213 g**
Green onions, cut into 1 inch (2.5 cm) pieces	**2**	**2**
Non-fat creamed cottage cheese	**³/₄ cup**	**175 mL**
Non-fat plain yogurt	**¹/₂ cup**	**125 mL**
Liquid smoke	**¹/₈ tsp.**	**0.5 mL**
Lemon juice	**2 tsp.**	**10 mL**
Freshly ground pepper, sprinkle		

Combine tomato juice and gelatin in small saucepan. Let stand for 5 minutes. Heat and stir on low until gelatin is dissolved. Set aside.

Process remaining 7 ingredients in food processor, scraping down sides as necessary, until smooth. Add gelatin mixture through chute. Mix well. Pour into lightly greased plastic-lined 2¹/₂ cup (625 mL) mold or deep bowl. Cover with plastic wrap. Chill for several hours until firm. To serve, turn out and remove wrap. Makes 2¹/₂ cups (625 mL).

NUTRITION INFORMATION 1 tbsp. (15 mL): 13 Calories; 0.3 g Total Fat (0.1 g Sat., 1.9 mg Cholesterol); 45 mg Sodium; 2 g Protein; 1 g Carbohydrate; trace Dietary Fiber

CHOICES Extra

Crispy Barbecue Chips

These don't have to be in wedges; they can be cut into irregular shapes. Pile in a bowl for a snack with friends. Try with Black Bean And Corn Salsa, below.

Spicy barbecue sauce	**1/3 cup**	**75 mL**
Olive oil	**2 tsp.**	**10 mL**
Sesame seeds	**2 tsp.**	**10 mL**
Garlic powder	**1/8 tsp.**	**0.5 mL**
Whole wheat flour tortillas (10 inch, 25 cm, size)	**4**	**4**

Combine first 4 ingredients in small dish.

Brush both sides of tortillas with barbecue sauce mixture. Cut each into 10 wedges. Arrange wedges in single layer on large greased baking sheet. Bake on bottom rack in 350°F (175°C) oven for 8 minutes. Turn wedges. Bake for 8 minutes until crispy and browned. Makes 40 chips.

NUTRITION INFORMATION 2 chips: 42 Calories; 0.8 g Total Fat (0.1 g Sat., 0 mg Cholesterol); 77 mg Sodium; 1 g Protein; 7 g Carbohydrate; trace Dietary Fiber

CHOICES 1/2 Starch

Pictured on front cover and on page 17.

Black Bean And Corn Salsa

Use the whole jalapeño for more of a hit. Use with Crispy Barbecue Chips, above.

Can of black beans, drained and rinsed	**19 oz.**	**540 mL**
Chopped red onion	**1/2 cup**	**125 mL**
Chopped fresh cilantro	**1 tbsp.**	**15 mL**
Diced jalapeño pepper, ribs and seeds removed (see Tip, page 101)	**1 tbsp.**	**15 mL**
Lime juice	**1 tbsp.**	**15 mL**
Ground cumin	**1/4 tsp.**	**1 mL**
Chili powder	**1/4 tsp.**	**1 mL**
Large tomato, chopped and seeded	**1**	**1**
Garlic clove, minced	**1**	**1**
Can of kernel corn, drained	**12 oz.**	**341 mL**
Salt	**1/2 tsp.**	**2 mL**

Combine all 11 ingredients in medium bowl. Cover. Chill for at least 2 hours to blend flavors. Makes 4 cups (1 L).

NUTRITION INFORMATION 1/4 cup (60 mL): 39 Calories; 0.2 g Total Fat (trace Sat., 0 mg Cholesterol); 167 mg Sodium; 2 g Protein; 8 g Carbohydrate; 1 g Dietary Fiber

CHOICES 1/2 Starch

Pictured on front cover and on page 17.

Sushi Layers

No bamboo mat or special technique required for these! They cut well and are easy to hold in your hands.

Water	4¹⁄₂ cups	1.1 L
Rice vinegar	¹⁄₃ cup	75 mL
Granulated sugar	¹⁄₄ cup	60 mL
Salt	1 tsp.	5 mL
Short grain (or pearl) rice	2¹⁄₄ cups	550 mL
Rice wine (sake) or dry sherry	¹⁄₄ cup	60 mL
Medium lemons, sliced paper-thin and seeded	2	2
Small capers, drained and rinsed	1 tbsp.	15 mL
Package of paper-thin slices smoked salmon	3 oz.	85 g
Small cooked shrimp	8 oz.	225 g
Nori sheets	4	4
Cucumber, with peel, thinly sliced (about ¹⁄₂ cucumber)	1¹⁄₂ cups	375 mL
Sliced green onion	¹⁄₂ cup	125 mL
Coarsely grated carrot	¹⁄₂ cup	125 mL
Large red pepper, diced	1	1

Bring water, vinegar, sugar and salt to a boil in medium saucepan. Stir in rice. Reduce heat. Cover. Simmer for 15 to 20 minutes until water is absorbed and rice is cooked. Stir in rice wine. Cool to room temperature. Makes about 8 cups (2 L) rice.

Line 9 × 13 inch (22 × 33 cm) pan with plastic wrap. Arrange thin even layer of lemon slices in bottom of pan. Sprinkle with capers. Cover ¹⁄₂ of pan with smoked salmon and ¹⁄₂ with shrimp. Using wet hands, pack about 2¹⁄₂ cups (625 mL) cooked rice in an even layer on top. Lay 2 sheets of nori, trimmed to fit in single layer, on rice.

Cover nori with cucumber and green onion. Pack 2¹⁄₂ cups (625 mL) rice on top. Layer carrot and red pepper. Cover with remaining rice. Lay 2 sheets of nori, trimmed to fit in single layer, on rice. Cover with plastic wrap directly on surface.

Set another 9 × 13 inch (22 × 33 cm) pan on sushi and press down firmly to compress layers evenly. Chill for 2 hours. Remove top plastic wrap. Invert sushi onto cutting surface. Remove remaining plastic wrap. Use sharp, wet, clean knife for each cut. Makes about sixty 1¹⁄₂ inch (3.8 cm) squares.

NUTRITION INFORMATION 1 square: 40 Calories; 0.2 g Total Fat (trace Sat., 7.6 mg Cholesterol); 85 mg Sodium; 2 g Protein; 8 g Carbohydrate; trace Dietary Fiber

CHOICES ¹⁄₂ Starch

Pictured on page 18.

Spicy Mexi-Bean Dip

Make this recipe to accompany Fresh Tomato Salsa, below. Serve both with Crispy Barbecue Chips, page 21.

Cooked (or 1 can, 19 oz., 540 mL) black beans, drained and rinsed	1½ cups	375 mL
Diced jalapeño pepper, ribs and seeds removed (see Tip, page 101)	1 tbsp.	15 mL
Salsa	¼ cup	60 mL
Light sour cream	¼ cup	60 mL
Grated light Monterey Jack cheese	1½ cups	375 mL

Mash beans with fork or masher until broken up. Add jalapeño, salsa, sour cream and ½ of cheese. Spoon into shallow 1 quart (1 L) casserole. Sprinkle remaining ½ of cheese on top. Bake, uncovered, in 350°F (175°C) oven for 20 minutes or until bubbly. Serve with baked tortilla chips. Makes 2 cups (500 mL).

NUTRITION INFORMATION 2 tbsp. (30 mL): 34 Calories; 1.8 g Total Fat (1.2 g Sat., 5.1 mg Cholesterol); 59 mg Sodium; 2 g Protein; 2 g Carbohydrate; trace Dietary Fiber

CHOICES ½ Starch; ½ Protein; ½ Fat & Oil

Pictured on page 17.

Fresh Tomato Salsa

Brightly colored and very fresh in flavor. A finely chopped jalapeño or other hot pepper could be added if you like it hot! Will keep for one day covered in refrigerator, but it will have much more liquid.

Diced, seeded roma (plum) tomatoes	2 cups	500 mL
Finely diced red onion	¼ cup	60 mL
Finely diced green pepper	¼ cup	60 mL
Garlic cloves, minced	2	2
Salt	¼ tsp.	1 mL
Freshly ground pepper, generous sprinkle		
Chopped fresh sweet basil (or 2 tsp., 10 mL, dried)	3 tbsp.	50 mL
Chopped fresh chives	1 tbsp.	15 mL
Red wine vinegar	1 tbsp.	15 mL
Chopped fresh cilantro (optional)	3 tbsp.	50 mL

Combine all 10 ingredients in medium bowl. Let stand at room temperature for at least 1 hour to blend flavors. Makes 2½ cups (625 mL).

NUTRITION INFORMATION 1 tbsp. (15 mL): 3 Calories; trace Total Fat (0 g Sat., 0 mg Cholesterol); 17 mg Sodium; trace Protein; 1 g Carbohydrate; trace Dietary Fiber

CHOICES Extra

Pictured on page 17 and on back cover.

Variation: Substitute balsamic vinegar for red wine vinegar for a deeper taste.

Piña Colada Smoothie

Has the color, flavor and texture of the real thing. Garnish with a slice of starfruit.

Can of crushed pineapple, with juice, chilled	**14 oz.**	**398 mL**
Coconut flavoring	**½ tsp.**	**2 mL**
Skim milk powder	**2 tbsp.**	**30 mL**
Non-fat vanilla yogurt	**1 cup**	**250 mL**
Ice cubes	**6**	**6**

Place first 4 ingredients in blender. Process on high, adding ice cubes, 1 at a time, through lid. As mixture becomes thick, use pulsing motion, scraping down sides occasionally, until smooth. Makes 4 cups (1 L).

NUTRITION INFORMATION ¾ cup (175 mL): 82 Calories; 0.1 g Total Fat (0.1 g Sat., 1.5 mg Cholesterol); 51 mg Sodium; 4 g Protein; 17 g Carbohydrate; 1 g Dietary Fiber

CHOICES 1 Fruit & Vegetable; 1 Milk

Pictured on page 17.

Sangria Refresher

Double this, and serve in a punch bowl with an ice ring at your next party. Garnish with slices of orange and lime.

Medium lime, very thinly sliced, seeded	**1**	**1**
Medium lemon, very thinly sliced, seeded	**1**	**1**
Medium oranges, very thinly sliced, seeded	**2**	**2**
Chopped fresh mint leaves (optional)	**¼ cup**	**60 mL**
Red grape juice	**1 qt.**	**1 L**
Sugar-free ginger ale	**1 qt.**	**1 L**

Place fruit and mint leaves in 2 quart (2 L) pitcher. Pour in grape juice. Chill for several hours or overnight to blend flavors.

Strain juice into large pitcher. Add ginger ale to taste. Makes 8 cups (2 L).

NUTRITION INFORMATION ½ cup (125 mL): 48 Calories; 0.1 g Total Fat (trace Sat., 0 mg Cholesterol); 6 mg Sodium; trace Protein; 12 g Carbohydrate; trace Dietary Fiber

CHOICES 1 Fruit & Vegetable

Pictured on front cover and on back cover.

 For pretty ice cubes, try freezing slices of fruit or berries in water. They can be used in summer-type cool drinks. Alternatively, freeze some of the punch, ice tea or sangria in cubes to keep the rest of drink chilled without diluting the drink.

Lemonberry Smoothie

A very refreshing snack. Sip it through a straw and maybe it will last longer!

Non-fat vanilla yogurt	1 cup	250 mL
Skim milk	1/4 cup	60 mL
Frozen concentrated lemonade	3 tbsp.	50 mL
Icing (confectioner's) sugar (or sugar substitute, such as Sugar Twin, to taste)	2 tsp.	10 mL
Frozen large whole strawberries	6	6

Place yogurt, milk, lemonade and sugar in blender. Process on high, adding strawberries, 1 at a time, through lid until thick. Process, scraping down sides as necessary, until smooth. Makes 2 1/2 cups (625 mL).

NUTRITION INFORMATION 3/4 cup (175 mL): 110 Calories; 0.2 g Total Fat (0.1 g Sat., 1.8 mg Cholesterol); 67 mg Sodium; 5 g Protein; 23 g Carbohydrate; 1 g Dietary Fiber

CHOICES 1 Fruit & Vegetable; 1 Milk; 1/2 Sugar

Pictured on page 71.

Pink Grapefruit Refresher

So refreshing! It will leave you wanting more. To serve as palate cleanser between courses, scrape with a meatball scoop and serve 3 balls per person in a tall glass.

Zest and juice from 3 medium oranges		
Zest and juice from 1 medium lemon		
Liquid honey	3 tbsp.	50 mL
Grand Marnier (or Triple Sec) liqueur (optional)	1/4 cup	60 mL
Water	1/4 cup	60 mL
Large pink grapefruits	5	5
Sugar-free lemon-lime soft drink	3 cups	750 mL
Grand Marnier (or Triple Sec) liqueur	1/4 cup	60 mL

Sugar-free lemon-lime soft drink, to taste

Cut zest from oranges and lemon with vegetable peeler into long, thin slivers. Place in small saucepan. Add fruit juices, honey, liqueur and water. Bring to a boil. Reduce heat to medium. Boil for 25 minutes until mixture is thickened and syrupy. Strain. Discard zest and pulp. Reserve syrup.

Halve and section grapefruits, discarding any seeds. Place sections in 9 x 13 inch (22 x 33 cm) glass baking pan. Scrape any remaining fruit from peel. Squeeze each half gently to drain any juices into pan. Add reserved syrup, soft drink and second amount of liqueur. Stir. Cover. Freeze for 2 hours. Break up with fork. Process in food processor or blender until smooth. Freeze. Makes 9 1/4 cups (2.3 L).

To serve, scoop about 1/2 cup (125 mL) into tall glass and fill with sugar-free lemon-lime soft drink.

NUTRITION INFORMATION 1/2 cup (125 mL) without soft drink: 67 Calories; 0.1 g Total Fat (trace Sat., 0 mg Cholesterol); 3 mg Sodium; 1 g Protein; 13 g Carbohydrate; trace Dietary Fiber

CHOICES 1 Fruit & Vegetable

Breads & Muffins

 erfect as a snack with a cup of tea or to complement lunch, these yeast breads, buns, quickbreads and muffins have been developed with reduced fat and sugar — and they're an excellent source of complex carbohydrates. These are the recipes that you will have success in cooking and pleasure in eating!

Cinnaraisin Nut Bread

Good grain and nut flavor in these dark loaves.

Large	1	1
Canola oil	1 tbsp.	15 mL
Brown sugar, packed	½ cup	125 mL
Salt	1 tsp.	5 mL
Ground cinnamon	1 tsp.	5 mL
Skim milk	2 cups	500 mL
Package of instant yeast (or 2¼ tsp., 11 mL, bulk)	¼ oz.	8 g
Whole wheat flour	1 cup	250 mL
Natural oat bran	½ cup	125 mL
Finely chopped toasted pecans	⅔ cup	150 mL
Seedless raisins	1 cup	250 mL
All-purpose flour	3¾ cups	925 mL

Whisk egg, canola oil, brown sugar, salt and cinnamon together in small bowl.

Heat skim milk until very warm. Whisk into egg mixture.

Combine yeast, whole wheat flour, oat bran and pecans in large bowl. Add milk mixture. Whisk until smooth. Stir in raisins. Slowly work in enough all-purpose flour until dough leaves sides of bowl and is no longer sticky. Turn out and knead on lightly floured surface for about 5 minutes until smooth and elastic. Place dough in greased bowl, turning once to coat top. Cover with tea towel. Let rise in oven with light on and door closed for about 1 hour until doubled in bulk. Punch down. Knead 8 to 10 times to remove air bubbles. Shape into 2 loaves. Place in 2 greased 9 x 5 x 3 inch (22 x 12.5 x 7.5 cm) loaf pans. Cover. Let rise until doubled in size. Bake in 375°F (190°C) oven for 35 to 40 minutes until hollow-sounding when tapped. Makes 2 loaves, for a total of 24 slices.

NUTRITION INFORMATION 1 slice: 176 Calories; 3.7 g Total Fat (0.4 g Sat., 9.4 mg Cholesterol); 130 mg Sodium; 5 g Protein; 33 g Carbohydrate; 2 g Dietary Fiber

CHOICES 1 Starch; 1 Fruit & Vegetable; ½ Milk; 1 Fat & Oil

Pictured on page 35.

Grain Bread

This loaf is very high in fiber but still light in texture.

Large eggs	2	2
Brown sugar, packed	¼ cup	60 mL
Fancy (mild) molasses	2 tbsp.	30 mL
Canola oil	½ cup	125 mL
1% buttermilk	1 qt.	1 L
Rolled oats (not instant)	1½ cups	375 mL
Light rye flour	1 cup	250 mL
Natural oat bran	½ cup	125 mL
Packages of instant yeast (¼ oz., 8 g, each) or 4½ tsp. (22 mL) bulk	2	2
Whole wheat flour	6¼ cups	1.5 L

Beat eggs, brown sugar, molasses and canola oil in large bowl.

Heat buttermilk in medium saucepan until very warm, almost hot. Whisk or beat into egg mixture until well-blended. Mixture should still be very warm.

Combine next 4 ingredients in small bowl. Mix into milk mixture until smooth. Let stand for 15 minutes.

Work or knead in enough whole wheat flour to make a sticky dough that keeps its form. Shape into 2 loaves. Place in greased 9 x 5 x 3 inch (22 x 12.5 x 7.5 cm) bread pan. Punch dough to fill in corners. Cover with greased waxed paper. Let rise in oven with door closed and light on for about 30 minutes until doubled in size. Bake in 350°F (175°C) oven for 40 minutes until hollow-sounding when tapped. Makes 2 loaves, for a total of 24 slices.

NUTRITION INFORMATION 1 slice: 236 Calories; 6.8 g Total Fat (1.8 g Sat., 39 mg Cholesterol); 54 mg Sodium; 8 g Protein; 38 g Carbohydrate; 6 g Dietary Fiber

CHOICES 2 Starch; 1 Milk; 1 Fat & Oil

Pictured on page 35.

GRAIN BUNS: Shape dough into 24 buns. Place in greased 9 x 13 inch (22 x 33 cm) pan. Cover with greased waxed paper. Let rise in oven with light on and door closed for approximately 1 hour until doubled in size. Bake in 350°F (175°C) oven for 20 minutes until hollow-sounding when tapped. Makes 24 buns.

The recipes in this cookbook use large eggs (when stated in the ingredients). If extra large eggs are used in breads, the liquid content will be higher which will cause the texture to be heavier; the extra liquid in cakes may cause them to fall when cooled.

Honey Wheat Bread

A slice of this bread is all you need for breakfast.

Very hot water	**1 cup**	**250 mL**
Liquid honey	**¼ cup**	**60 mL**
Canola oil	**2 tbsp.**	**30 mL**
Salt	**1 tsp.**	**5 mL**
Large egg, fork-beaten	**1**	**1**
All-purpose flour	**2 cups**	**500 mL**
Package of instant yeast (or 2¼ tsp., 11 mL, bulk)	**¼ oz.**	**8 g**
Whole wheat flour	**1¼ cups**	**300 mL**
Chopped dried fruit (or raisins)	**½ cup**	**125 mL**

Combine water, honey, canola oil and salt in small bowl.

Put egg into large bowl. Slowly add hot water mixture, whisking until frothy.

Combine all-purpose flour and yeast in small bowl. Add to liquids. Mix well until smooth.

Slowly add whole wheat flour. Mix until soft dough is formed. Add more or less flour, as required, until soft but not too sticky.

Turn out and knead on floured surface for 10 minutes, adding dried fruit gradually, until smooth and elastic. Place in greased bowl, turning once to coat top. Cover with tea towel. Let rise in oven with light on and door closed for 1½ hours until doubled in bulk. Punch down. Shape into loaf. Place in greased 9 x 5 x 3 inch (22 x 12.5 x 7.5 cm) loaf pan. Cover. Let rise until almost doubled in size. Bake in 350°F (175°C) oven for 40 to 45 minutes until hollow-sounding when tapped. If top browns too quickly, cover with foil or brown paper for last 10 minutes of baking time. Makes 1 loaf, enough for 12 slices.

NUTRITION INFORMATION 1 slice: 195 Calories; 3.2 g Total Fat (0.4 g Sat., 18 mg Cholesterol); 234 mg Sodium; 5 g Protein; 38 g Carbohydrate; 3 g Dietary Fiber

CHOICES 1½ Starch; ½ Fruit & Vegetable; 1 Sugar; ½ Fat & Oil

Pictured on page 35.

To test yeast for freshness, sprinkle some over warm water that has a little sugar in it. If the solution foams and bubbles, it's still active. If not, replace with new yeast.

Cloverleaf Honey Rolls

Good, wholesome buns.

Skim milk	1⅓ cups	325 mL
Hard margarine	⅓ cup	75 mL
Liquid honey	¼ cup	60 mL
Salt	1 tsp.	5 mL
Whole wheat flour	2 cups	500 mL
All-purpose flour	1 cup	250 mL
Packages of instant yeast (¼ oz., 8 g, each), or 4½ tsp., 22 mL, bulk	2	2
Frozen egg product, thawed (see Note)	6 tbsp.	100 mL
All-purpose flour	2 cups	500 mL

Heat first 4 ingredients in small saucepan until margarine is melted and mixture is very warm but not hot.

Combine whole wheat and first amount of all-purpose flour with yeast in large bowl. Add wet ingredients. Beat well. Add egg product. Beat.

Add all-purpose flour, 1 cup (250 mL) at a time. Work in by mixing and kneading until soft dough is formed. Turn out and knead on floured surface for 5 to 10 minutes until dough is smooth and elastic. Place in greased bowl, turning once to coat top. Cover with tea towel. Let rise in oven with light on and door closed for 1 hour until doubled in size. Punch down. Divide dough into 4 equal portions. Work with 1 portion at a time, keeping remainder covered. Shape into long roll. Cut into 9 pieces. Cut piece into 3 smaller pieces. Roll into small balls. Place 3 balls in each greased muffin cup. Repeat with remaining portions. Cover with tea towel. Let rise in oven with light on and door closed for 60 minutes until doubled in size. Bake in 400°F (205°C) oven for 10 minutes until golden brown. Makes 3 dozen rolls.

NUTRITION INFORMATION 1 roll: 94 Calories; 2.1 g Total Fat (0.4 g Sat., 0.2 mg Cholesterol); 109 mg Sodium; 3 g Protein; 16 g Carbohydrate; 1 g Dietary Fiber

CHOICES 1 Starch; ½ Fat & Oil

Note: 4 tbsp. (50 mL) =1 large egg

To further cut down on fat grams, lightly spray muffin cups with no-stick cooking spray or use paper muffin liners.

Onion Cheese Biscuits

Delicious warm with soup or salad, or just some fresh fruit.

All-purpose flour	1 cup	250 mL
Whole wheat flour	1 cup	250 mL
Baking powder	2 tsp.	10 mL
Baking soda	1/2 tsp.	2 mL
Grated light sharp Cheddar cheese	1 cup	250 mL
Dill weed	1 tsp.	5 mL
Salt	1/4 tsp.	1 mL
Freshly ground pepper	1/8 tsp.	0.5 mL
Non-fat plain yogurt	3/4 cup	175 mL
Skim milk	1/2 cup	125 mL
Canola oil	2 tbsp.	30 mL
Green onions, with tops, chopped	4	4

Combine first 8 ingredients in large bowl.

Combine remaining 4 ingredients in small bowl. Add to flour mixture. Stir just until dry ingredients are moistened. Drop by large spoonfuls onto greased baking sheet. Bake in center of 400°F (205°C) oven for 12 to 15 minutes until golden brown. Makes 12 biscuits.

NUTRITION INFORMATION 1 biscuit: 140 Calories; 4.6 g Total Fat (1.5 g Sat., 6.5 mg Cholesterol); 199 mg Sodium; 6 g Protein; 18 g Carbohydrate; 2 g Dietary Fiber

CHOICES 1 Starch; 1/2 Milk; 1/2 Protein; 1/2 Fat & Oil

Pictured on page 35 and on back cover.

Chili 'N' Cheese Corn Muffins

So good with soup. Chilies and chili powder give a spicy aftertaste.

Yellow cornmeal	3/4 cup	175 mL
1% buttermilk	1 cup	250 mL
Large eggs, fork-beaten	2	2
Can of diced green chilies, with liquid	4 oz.	114 mL
Canola oil	1 1/2 tbsp.	25 mL
All-purpose flour	1 1/2 cups	375 mL
Baking powder	1 tbsp.	15 mL
Salt	1/2 tsp.	2 mL
Brown sugar, packed	2 tbsp.	30 mL
Chili powder	1/4-1/2 tsp.	1-2 mL
Grated light sharp Cheddar cheese	3/4 cup	175 mL

(continued on next page)

Mix cornmeal, buttermilk, eggs, chilies and canola oil. Let stand for 15 minutes.

Mix remaining 6 ingredients in large bowl. Make a well in center. Pour cornmeal mixture into well. Stir just until moistened. Spray muffin cups with no-stick cooking spray. Fill cups ¾ full. Bake in 375°F (190°C) oven for 20 minutes until wooden pick inserted in center of muffin comes out clean. Cool in pan for 5 minutes before turning out. Makes 12 muffins.

NUTRITION INFORMATION 1 muffin: 166 Calories; 4.6 g Total Fat (1.5 g Sat., 41.2 mg Cholesterol); 311 mg Sodium; 6 g Protein; 24 g Carbohydrate; 1 g Dietary Fiber

CHOICES 1 Starch; 1 Milk; 1 Fat & Oil

Pictured on page 35.

Cornbread Muffins

The bits of corn give off a touch of sweetness. Makes a big batch. These freeze well and can be warmed for lunch.

Yellow cornmeal	**1½ cups**	**375 mL**
1% buttermilk	**1⅓ cups**	**325 mL**
All-purpose flour	**3 cups**	**750 mL**
Brown sugar, packed	**¼ cup**	**60 mL**
Baking powder	**2 tbsp.**	**30 mL**
Salt	**1 tsp.**	**5 mL**
Frozen egg product, thawed (see Note)	**1 cup**	**250 mL**
Canola oil	**⅓ cup**	**75 mL**
Can of cream-style corn	**14 oz.**	**398 mL**

Combine cornmeal and buttermilk in medium bowl. Let rest for 15 minutes.

Combine flour, brown sugar, baking powder and salt in medium bowl. Make a well in center.

Mix egg product, canola oil and corn in small bowl. Add to cornmeal mixture. Mix well. Pour into well. Stir just until moistened. Spray muffin cups with no-stick cooking spray. Fill cups ¾ full. Bake in 375°F (190°C) oven for 15 to 17 minutes until wooden pick inserted in center of muffin comes out clean. Cool in pan for 5 minutes before turning out. Makes 24 muffins.

NUTRITION INFORMATION 1 muffin: 157 Calories; 3.8 g Total Fat (0.4 g Sat., 0.5 mg Cholesterol); 205 mg Sodium; 4 g Protein; 27 g Carbohydrate; 1 g Dietary Fiber

CHOICES 1 Starch; ½ Fruit & Vegetable; ½ Milk; 1 Fat & Oil

Note: 4 tbsp. (50 mL) =1 large egg

Orange Date Muffins

Great orange aroma and flavor. Bits of dates and raisins give sweetness.

All-purpose flour	1½ cups	375 mL
Brown sugar, packed	2 tbsp.	30 mL
Baking soda	1 tsp.	5 mL
Baking powder	1 tsp.	5 mL
Salt	¼ tsp.	1 mL
Medium orange, with peel, cut into 8 pieces	1	1
Light raisins (optional)	¼ cup	60 mL
Chopped dates	¼ cup	60 mL
1% buttermilk	⅔ cup	150 mL
Canola oil	3 tbsp.	50 mL
Frozen egg product, thawed (see Note)	6 tbsp.	100 mL

Combine first 5 ingredients in medium bowl. Make a well in center.

Combine remaining 6 ingredients in blender. Process until orange, raisins and dates are well-chopped. Pour into well. Stir just until moistened. Spray muffin cups with no-stick cooking spray. Fill cups ¾ full. Bake in 400°F (205°C) oven for 18 to 20 minutes until wooden pick inserted in center of muffin comes out clean. Cool in pan for 5 minutes before turning out. Makes 12 muffins.

NUTRITION INFORMATION 1 muffin: 135 Calories; 3.9 g Total Fat (0.4 g Sat., 0.5 mg Cholesterol); 209 mg Sodium; 4 g Protein; 23 g Carbohydrate; 2 g Dietary Fiber

CHOICES 1 Starch; 1 Fruit & Vegetable; 1 Fat & Oil

Pictured on page 35.

Note: 4 tbsp. (50 mL) =1 large egg

Carrot Pineapple Muffins

A very moist muffin with a definite pineapple flavor.

All-purpose flour	1⅓ cups	325 mL
Quick-cooking rolled oats (not instant)	1 cup	250 mL
Brown sugar, packed	½ cup	125 mL
Baking powder	1½ tbsp.	25 mL
Ground cinnamon	½ tsp.	2 mL
Salt	¼ tsp.	1 mL
Ground nutmeg	⅛ tsp.	0.5 mL
Frozen egg product, thawed (see Note)	¼ cup	60 mL
Canola oil	¼ cup	60 mL
Non-fat vanilla yogurt	½ cup	125 mL
Can of crushed pineapple, well-drained	8 oz.	227 mL
Grated carrot	½ cup	125 mL

(continued on next page)

Combine first 7 ingredients in large bowl. Make a well in center.

Mix remaining 5 ingredients in small bowl. Pour into well. Stir just until moistened. Spray muffin cups with no-stick cooking spray. Fill cups ³/₄ full. Bake in 400°F (205°C) oven for 20 minutes until wooden pick inserted in center of muffin comes out clean. Cool in pan for 5 minutes before turning out. Makes 12 muffins.

NUTRITION INFORMATION 1 muffin: 182 Calories; 5.6 g Total Fat (0.5 g Sat., 0.2 mg Cholesterol); 86 mg Sodium; 4 g Protein; 30 g Carbohydrate; 2 g Dietary Fiber

CHOICES 1 Starch; 1 Fruit & Vegetable; 1 Sugar; 1 Fat & Oil

Note: 4 tbsp. (50 mL) =1 large egg

Cranberry Streusel Muffins

Use orange pulp in the juice measurement for added flavor. Moist, tender and pretty — besides being very, very good!

All-purpose flour	**2 cups**	**500 mL**
Granulated sugar	**¹/₂ cup**	**125 mL**
Baking powder	**1 tbsp.**	**15 mL**
Salt	**¹/₂ tsp.**	**2 mL**
Egg whites (large)	**4**	**4**
Hard margarine, melted	**3 tbsp.**	**50 mL**
Freshly squeezed orange juice (pulp, optional)	**1 cup**	**250 mL**
Grated orange peel	**2 tsp.**	**10 mL**
Chopped dried cranberries	**²/₃ cup**	**150 mL**
STREUSEL TOPPING		
All-purpose flour	**¹/₄ cup**	**60 mL**
Brown sugar, packed	**1 tbsp.**	**15 mL**
Hard margarine	**1 tbsp.**	**15 mL**

Combine first 4 ingredients in medium bowl. Make a well in center.

Beat egg whites, margarine, orange juice and peel in small bowl until combined. Stir in cranberries. Pour into well. Stir just until moistened. Spray muffin cups with no-stick cooking spray. Fill cups ³/₄ full.

Streusel Topping: Combine flour and brown sugar in small bowl. Cut in margarine until mixture is crumbly. Sprinkle ¹/₂ tbsp. (7 mL) over each muffin. Bake in 425°F (220°C) oven for 10 to 15 minutes until just firm. Do not overbake. Cool in pan for 5 minutes before turning out. Makes 12 muffins.

NUTRITION INFORMATION 1 muffin: 190 Calories; 4 g Total Fat (0.8 g Sat., 0 mg Cholesterol); 179 mg Sodium; 4 g Protein; 35 g Carbohydrate; 2 g Dietary Fiber

CHOICES 1 Starch; 1 Fruit & Vegetable; 1 Sugar; 1 Fat & Oil

Pictured on page 35.

Pumpkin Raisin Muffins

Raisins in every bite in these spiced muffins.

All-purpose flour	1 cup	250 mL
Whole wheat flour	¾ cup	175 mL
Natural oat bran	¼ cup	60 mL
Brown sugar, packed	½ cup	125 mL
Baking soda	1½ tsp.	7 mL
Baking powder	1 tsp.	5 mL
Ground cinnamon	1 tsp.	5 mL
Ground nutmeg	½ tsp.	2 mL
Ground allspice	¼ tsp.	1 mL
Salt	¼ tsp.	1 mL
Can of pumpkin (without spices)	14 oz.	398 mL
Large egg, fork-beaten	1	1
Skim milk	1 cup	250 mL
Canola oil	2 tbsp.	30 mL
Freshly grated lemon peel	1 tsp.	5 mL
Raisins	1 cup	250 mL

Combine first 10 ingredients in large bowl. Make a well in center.

Beat together next 5 ingredients in medium bowl until smooth. Pour into well. Stir until barely combined Add raisins. Stir just until moistened. Spray muffin cups with no-stick cooking spray. Fill cups ¾ full. Bake in 400°F (205°C) oven for 20 minutes until wooden pick inserted in center of muffin comes out clean. Cool in pan for 5 minutes before turning out. Makes 12 muffins.

NUTRITION INFORMATION 1 muffin: 194 Calories; 3.4 g Total Fat (0.5 g Sat., 18.4 mg Cholesterol); 196 mg Sodium; 5 g Protein; 39 g Carbohydrate; 3 g Dietary Fiber

CHOICES 1 Starch; 1½ Fruit & Vegetable; 1 Sugar; 1 Fat & Oil

Pictured on page 35.

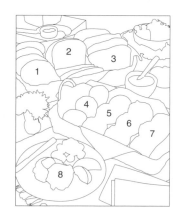

Oatmeal Apple Muffins

Nice texture with bits of apple. A good breakfast or snack.

Whole wheat flour	1¼ cups	300 mL
Quick-cooking rolled oats (not instant)	1 cup	250 mL
Brown sugar, packed	⅓ cup	75 mL
Baking powder	2½ tsp.	12 mL
Baking soda	¼ tsp.	1 mL
Salt	¼ tsp.	1 mL
Ground nutmeg	¼ tsp.	1 mL
Ground cinnamon	¼ tsp.	1 mL
1% buttermilk	1 cup	250 mL
Large egg, fork-beaten	1	1
Canola oil	2 tbsp.	30 mL
Medium apple, peeled and diced	1	1

Combine first 8 ingredients in large bowl. Make a well in center.

Combine next 3 ingredients in small bowl. Pour into well. Add apple. Stir just until moistened. Spray muffin cups with no-stick cooking spray. Measure about ¼ cup (60 mL) into each cup. Bake in 375°F (190°C) oven for 15 to 18 minutes until wooden pick inserted in center of muffin comes out clean. Cool in pan for 5 minutes before turning out. Makes 12 muffins.

NUTRITION INFORMATION 1 muffin: 139 Calories; 3.7 g Total Fat (0.6 g Sat., 18.7 mg Cholesterol); 119 mg Sodium; 4 g Protein; 24 g Carbohydrate; 3 g Dietary Fiber

CHOICES 1 Starch; ½ Fruit & Vegetable; ½ Sugar; ½ Fat & Oil

1. Apple Clafouti, page 42
2. G'Morning Pizza, page 39
3. Morning Burritos, page 43

· B R E A D S   A N D   M U F F I N S ·

Breakfast

Check out these choices to spice up your mornings! This section offers some palate-pleasing recipes that are high in fiber and complex carbohydrates but low in fat. If you're tired of the same old cereal and milk to start your day, try G' Morning Pizza, page 39, or Morning Burritos, page 43. For people with diabetes, every meal is important, but breakfast provides a good start to everyone's day. Let it be delicious!

Ham 'N' Apple Strata

Golden crisp topping with layers of ham, apple and bread.

Whole wheat bread slices, crusts removed	8	8
Fat-free ham slices (or lean back bacon)	4½ oz.	125 g
Large apple, cored and cut into thin wedges	1	1
Grated light sharp Cheddar cheese	½ cup	125 mL
Carton of frozen egg product, thawed (see Note)	8 oz.	227 mL
Egg whites (large)	4	4
Skim evaporated milk	1 cup	250 mL
Water	½ cup	125 mL
Seasoned salt	½ tsp.	2 mL
Hot pepper sauce	¼ tsp.	1 mL
Corn flakes cereal	1 cup	250 mL
Margarine, melted	1 tbsp.	15 mL
Grated light sharp Cheddar cheese	½ cup	125 mL

Place 4 slices of bread in greased shallow 2 quart (2 L) casserole or 9 x 9 inch (22 x 22 cm) pan. Layer bread with ham, apple wedges and first amount of cheese. Cover with remaining 4 bread slices.

Beat next 6 ingredients together. Slowly pour onto bread slices. Cover tightly with plastic wrap. Chill overnight.

Crush cereal in small bowl. Add margarine and second amount of cheese. Stir. Sprinkle over strata. Bake, uncovered, in 350°F (175°C) oven for 50 to 55 minutes until set and top is golden brown. Let stand for 15 minutes before cutting. Cuts into 4 pieces.

NUTRITION INFORMATION 1 piece: 412 Calories; 10.8 g Total Fat (4.7 g Sat., 22 mg Cholesterol); 1367 mg Sodium; 32 g Protein; 49 g Carbohydrate; 4 g Dietary Fiber

CHOICES 2 Starch; ½ Fruit & Vegetable; 2 Milk; 2½ Protein; ½ Fat & Oil

Note: 4 tbsp. (50 mL) =1 large egg

G' Morning Pizza

A nice brunch for the whole family.

All-purpose flour	1 cup	250 mL
Whole wheat flour	½ cup	125 mL
Instant yeast	1½ tsp.	7 mL
Grated light Parmesan cheese	1 tbsp.	15 mL
Dried sweet basil	½ tsp.	2 mL
Dried whole oregano	¼ tsp.	1 mL
Salt	½ tsp.	2 mL
Very warm water	⅔ cup	150 mL
Canola oil	2 tsp.	10 mL
Large hard-boiled eggs, peeled	6	6
Light cream cheese	4 oz.	125 g
Parsley flakes	½ tsp.	2 mL
Dried sweet basil	½ tsp.	2 mL
Garlic powder	1/16 tsp.	0.5 mL
Fat-free ham slices, diced	⅔ cup	150 mL
Grated part-skim mozzarella cheese	1 cup	250 mL
Thinly sliced red onion	½ cup	125 mL
Thinly sliced green and red peppers	⅔ cup	150 mL
Dried sweet basil, sprinkle (optional)		
Dried whole oregano, sprinkle (optional)		

Combine first 7 ingredients in food processor or medium bowl.

Combine water and canola oil in small bowl. Add through chute while processing until dough forms ball (or if mixing in bowl, stir in water and canola oil until dough leaves sides of bowl). Turn out and knead for 3 to 4 minutes until smooth. Cover. Let stand for 15 minutes. Press lightly in greased 12 inch (30 cm) pizza pan. Form raised rim around edge. Bake in 425°F (220°C) oven for 8 minutes, poking any bubbles with fork.

Discard 4 yolks. Chop remaining egg whites and 2 whole eggs.

Mix cream cheese with parsley, basil and garlic powder. Spread onto hot crust. Layer with eggs, ham, cheese, red onion and peppers. Sprinkle with basil and oregano. Bake in center of 425°F (220°C) oven for 8 to 10 minutes until cheese is melted and crust is browned. Cuts into 8 wedges.

NUTRITION INFORMATION 1 wedge: 215 Calories; 8 g Total Fat (2.9 g Sat., 66.4 mg Cholesterol); 648 mg Sodium; 13 g Protein; 23 g Carbohydrate; 2 g Dietary Fiber

CHOICES 1½ Starch; 1 Protein; 1 Fat & Oil

Pictured on page 36.

Buttermilk Pancakes

Serve with Blueberry Sauce, page 41, or Danish Cream Topping, below, for a special treat.

Whole wheat flour	¾ cup	175 mL
All-purpose flour	¾ cup	175 mL
Brown sugar, packed	2 tbsp.	30 mL
Baking powder	1 tbsp.	15 mL
Baking soda	½ tsp.	2 mL
Salt	¼ tsp.	1 mL
1% buttermilk	1½ cups	375 mL
Egg yolks (large)	2	2
Canola oil	3 tbsp.	50 mL
Egg whites (large)	2	2

Combine first 6 ingredients in medium bowl.

Whisk buttermilk, egg yolks and canola oil in small bowl. Add to dry ingredients. Stir just until moistened. Batter will be lumpy.

Beat egg whites in small bowl until stiff. Fold into batter. Pour batter into non-stick frying pan. Cook on medium-low for 3 to 5 minutes per side until golden brown. Makes 12 pancakes.

NUTRITION INFORMATION 1 pancake: 123 Calories; 4.8 g Total Fat (0.7 g Sat., 37.1 mg Cholesterol); 164 mg Sodium; 4 g Protein; 16 g Carbohydrate; 1 g Dietary Fiber

CHOICES 1 Starch; ½ Milk; ½ Fat & Oil

Danish Cream Topping

Great on Buttermilk Pancakes, above, and any whole grain toast or bagel. Freezes well.

Non-fat creamed cottage cheese	2 cups	500 mL
Skim milk	2 tbsp.	30 mL
Liquid honey	1 tbsp.	15 mL
Finely grated orange peel	½ tsp.	2 mL
Ground cinnamon	¼ tsp.	1 mL
Almond flavoring	¼ tsp.	1 mL

Place all 6 ingredients in blender. Process for 2 minutes, scraping down sides as necessary, until puréed. Makes 2 cups (500 mL).

NUTRITION INFORMATION 2 tbsp. (30 mL): 30 Calories; trace Total Fat (0 g Sat., trace Cholesterol); 54 mg Sodium; 5 g Protein; 2 g Carbohydrate; trace Dietary Fiber

CHOICES 1 Protein; Extra

Blueberry Sauce

This is very good with Buttermilk Pancakes, page 40.

Fresh (or frozen, thawed) blueberries	**3 cups**	**750 mL**
Unsweetened apple (or pineapple) juice	**¹/₂ cup**	**125 mL**
Cornstarch	**4 tsp.**	**20 mL**
Cold water	**2 tbsp.**	**30 ml**
Lemon juice	**1 tsp.**	**5 mL**
Vanilla	**¹/₂ tsp.**	**2 mL**
Sugar substitute (such as Sugar Twin)	**2 tbsp.**	**30 mL**

Place blueberries and apple juice in medium saucepan. Simmer on medium about 4 to 8 minutes until blueberries start to break apart and are soft.

Combine cornstarch with water in small dish. Stir into blueberries. Bring to a boil. Boil for about 2 minutes on low until clear and thickened. Remove from heat.

Stir in lemon juice, vanilla and sugar substitute. Serve warm or at room temperature. Makes 2 cups (500 mL).

NUTRITION INFORMATION ¹/₄ cup (60 mL): 46 Calories; 0.2 g Total Fat (0 g Sat., 0 mg Cholesterol); 4 mg Sodium; trace Protein; 11 g Carbohydrate; 2 g Dietary Fiber

CHOICES 1 Fruit & Vegetable

Hot Wheat Berry Pudding

Satisfies your chewy cravings with nice sweetness. Serve with milk or yogurt.

Wheat berries (unprocessed wheat kernels)	**1¹/₄ cups**	**300 mL**
Water	**4¹/₄ cups**	**1 L**
Mixture of raisins and dried fruits, chopped if large	**1 cup**	**250 mL**
Long thread (or flake) coconut	**¹/₃ cup**	**75 mL**
Coarsely chopped almonds	**¹/₄ cup**	**60 mL**
Brown sugar, packed	**3 tbsp.**	**50 mL**

Cook wheat berries in water in large saucepan for 1¹/₄ hours until wheat is tender but still quite chewy.

Stir in dried fruits, coconut, almonds and brown sugar. Let stand for 5 minutes. Makes 4 cups (1 L).

NUTRITION INFORMATION ¹/₂ cup (125 mL): 254 Calories; 5.4 g Total Fat (2.6 g Sat., 1.2 mg Cholesterol); 53 mg Sodium; 9 g Protein; 47 g Carbohydrate; 5 g Dietary Fiber

CHOICES 1 Starch; 2 Fruit & Vegetable; 1 Milk; ¹/₂ Sugar; 1 Fat & Oil

Apple Clafouti

Custard consistency with crunchy apples.

Large cooking apple (such as McIntosh), peeled, cored and cut into thin wedges	1	1
Light raisins (or fresh cranberries)	¼ cup	60 mL
Brown sugar, packed	2 tbsp.	30 mL
Ground cinnamon	¼ tsp.	1 mL
Skim milk	1¼ cups	300 mL
Canola oil	1 tbsp.	15 mL
Frozen egg product, thawed (see Note)	½ cup	125 mL
Vanilla	1 tsp.	5 mL
Whole wheat flour	⅓ cup	75 mL
All-purpose flour	⅓ cup	75 mL
Granulated sugar	¼ cup	60 mL
Ground cinnamon	¼ tsp.	1 mL

Overlap apple wedges in circle in bottom of well-greased 9 inch (22 cm) glass pie plate. Sprinkle with raisins, brown sugar and cinnamon.

Beat milk, canola oil, egg product and vanilla in medium bowl. Add both flours, granulated sugar and cinnamon. Beat until smooth. Spread batter evenly over apple. Bake in center of 375°F (190°C) oven for 40 minutes until set and golden brown. To serve, invert (so apples will be on top) onto plate. Cuts into 6 wedges.

NUTRITION INFORMATION 1 wedge: 187 Calories; 2.8 g Total Fat (0.3 g Sat., 1 mg Cholesterol); 71 mg Sodium; 6 g Protein; 36 g Carbohydrate; 2 g Dietary Fiber

CHOICES 1 Starch; 1 Fruit & Vegetable; 1 Sugar; ½ Protein

Pictured on page 36.

Note: 4 tbsp. (50 mL) =1 large egg

Baked Omelet Puff

Layered look when cut. Removes easily in wedges.

Margarine	1 tsp.	5 mL
Finely diced red pepper	¼ cup	60 mL
Sliced green onion	¼ cup	60 mL
Diced zucchini, with peel	½ cup	125 mL
Sliced fresh mushrooms	½ cup	125 mL
Salt	½ tsp.	2 mL
Freshly ground pepper, generous sprinkle		
Large eggs, separated	4	4
Egg whites (large)	4	4
Grated light sharp Cheddar cheese	½ cup	125 mL
Paprika, sprinkle		

(continued on next page)

Heat margarine in medium non-stick fry pan until bubbling. Add next 4 ingredients. Stir. Cook on medium-high until liquid has evaporated. Stir in salt and pepper. Cool to room temperature.

Beat egg yolks in small bowl until thick and lemon-colored. Stir into vegetables.

Beat egg whites from 8 eggs with clean beaters in large bowl until soft peaks form. Gently fold in vegetable mixture and cheese. Pour into well-greased 10 inch (25 cm) glass pie plate or 2 quart (2 L) casserole. Sprinkle with paprika. Bake in 350°F (175°C) oven for about 25 minutes until knife inserted in center comes out clean. Cuts into 8 wedges.

NUTRITION INFORMATION 1 wedge: 77 Calories; 4.5 g Total Fat (2.4 g Sat., 149.6 mg Cholesterol); 283 mg Sodium; 7 g Protein; 2 g Carbohydrate; trace Dietary Fiber

CHOICES 1 Protein; 1 Fat & Oil

Morning Burritos

Makes a great breakfast for the whole family. Serve with fresh fruit.

Chopped green onion	¼ **cup**	**60 mL**
Margarine	**2 tsp.**	**10 mL**
Frozen egg product, thawed (see Note)	**1 cup**	**250 mL**
Chili powder	¼ **tsp.**	**1 mL**
Salt	¼ **tsp.**	**1 mL**
Chopped pickled hot peppers	**2 tbsp.**	**30 mL**
Grated light aged Cheddar (or Monterey Jack) cheese	¾ **cup**	**175 mL**
Whole wheat flour tortillas (10 inch, 25 cm, size), warmed	**4**	**4**
Salsa (optional)	**2 tbsp.**	**30 mL**
Light sour cream (optional)	**2 tbsp.**	**30 mL**

Sauté green onion in margarine in large non-stick frying pan for 30 seconds. Pour in egg product. Sprinkle with chili powder and salt. Heat, stirring occasionally, on medium until eggs start to set. Add peppers. Heat until eggs are cooked.

Divide and sprinkle cheese over tortillas. Place ¼ of egg mixture in line down center of each tortilla over cheese. Top eggs with salsa and sour cream. Roll tortillas, tucking in sides, to enclose filling. Cut in half to serve. Makes 4 burritos.

NUTRITION INFORMATION 1 burrito: 284 Calories; 7.6 g Total Fat (3.4 g Sat., 13.5 mg Cholesterol); 705 mg Sodium; 18 g Protein; 35 g Carbohydrate; 1 g Dietary Fiber

CHOICES 2 Starch; 2 Protein; ½ Fat & Oil

Pictured on page 36.

Note: 4 tbsp. (50 mL) =1 large egg

• B R E A K F A S T •

Desserts

t's no fun declining treats when everyone else is enjoying them. There was a time when people with diabetes were told to avoid sugar at all costs. But now they can have their cake and eat it too, thanks to the new dietary guidelines. With some planning, you can fit these yummy desserts into your daily requirements, and at the same time satisfy your sweet tooth. Remember, indulge, don't overindulge.

Lemon Angel Tower

This makes an elegant birthday cake. A serrated knife works best to cut angel food cake.

Package of angel food cake mix	**16 oz.**	**450 g**
FROSTING		
Package of lemon-flavored gelatin (jelly powder), see Note	**3 oz.**	**85 g**
Boiling water	**¹/₂ cup**	**125 mL**
Non-fat lemon yogurt	**³/₄ cup**	**175 mL**
Light liquid topping (such as Nutriwhip)	**1 cup**	**250 mL**

Grated zest from 1 medium lemon
Strips of lemon peel, for garnish

Prepare angel food cake as per package directions. Cool completely. Slice horizontally twice to make 3 equal layers.

Frosting: Dissolve jelly powder in boiling water in small bowl. Whisk in yogurt until smooth. Chill about 30 minutes, stirring every 10 minutes, until syrupy.

Beat topping until stiff peaks form. Add lemon zest. Gradually add yogurt mixture while beating. Chill for about 40 minutes, folding several times, until set to spreadable consistency. Makes 6 cups (1.5 L) frosting.

Fill each layer with about 1¹/₂ cups (375 mL) frosting. Use remaining frosting to cover top and sides of cake. Garnish with lemon peel. Chill. Cuts into 10 wedges.

NUTRITION INFORMATION ¹/₂ wedge: 234 Calories; 1.2 g Total Fat (1 g Sat., 0.4 mg Cholesterol); 126 mg Sodium; 6 g Protein; 51 g Carbohydrate; trace Dietary Fiber
CHOICES 2 Starch; 2 Sugar

Note: To further reduce sugar, use sugar-free lemon-flavored gelatin (jelly powder).

Almond Cheesecake

Good cheesecake texture and flavor. The variation with fresh fruit is delicious as well.

CRUST		
Digestive biscuit crumbs (about 8 biscuits)	1¼ cups	300 mL
Ground almonds	¼ cup	60 mL
Margarine, melted	2 tbsp.	30 mL
Water	1 tbsp.	15 mL
FILLING		
Envelopes of unflavored gelatin (¼ oz., 7 g, each)	2	2
Skim milk	¼ cup	60 mL
1% buttermilk	1¼ cups	300 mL
Part-skim ricotta cheese	1½ cups	375 mL
Sugar substitute (such as Sugar Twin)	¼-⅓ cup	60-75 mL
Almond flavoring	½ tsp.	2 mL
Light frozen whipped topping, thawed	2 cups	500 mL
Sliced almonds, toasted	2 tbsp.	30 mL

Crust: Combine biscuit crumbs, almonds and margarine in small bowl. Add water, 1 tsp. (5 mL) at a time, until crumbs stick together when squeezed. Press firmly into greased 9 inch (22 cm) springform pan. Bake in 325°F (160°C) oven for 10 minutes. Cool.

Filling: Stir gelatin and milk in small dish. Let stand for 5 minutes. Microwave on high (100%) for 10 seconds or heat over hot water. Stir to dissolve gelatin. Let stand at room temperature to cool slightly but still remain liquid. See Tip, page 47.

Beat buttermilk, ricotta cheese, sugar substitute and flavoring in large bowl for several minutes until light and frothy. Beat in gelatin mixture. Fold in whipped topping. Pour into crust.

Sprinkle with almonds, pressing in slightly. Cover. Chill for several hours or overnight until firm. Cuts into 10 wedges.

NUTRITION INFORMATION 1 wedge: 209 Calories; 11.1 g Total Fat (5.1 g Sat., 13.3 mg Cholesterol); 213 mg Sodium; 9 g Protein; 20 g Carbohydrate; 1 g Dietary Fiber

CHOICES 1 Starch; ½ Sugar; 1 Protein; 1 Fat & Oil

LEMON CHEESECAKE: Omit almond flavoring. Add ½ tsp. (2 mL) lemon flavoring. Fold 1 tsp. (5 mL) grated lemon peel and whipped topping into filling. Serve with Fresh Fruit Salad, page 60.

Mocha Nut Meringues

Individual desserts for ten special guests.

Cocoa	2 tsp.	10 mL
Icing (confectioner's) sugar	3 tbsp.	50 mL
Instant coffee granules, ground to fine powder (see Tip, below)	1½ tsp.	7 mL
Vanilla Yogurt Cheese, page 75	2¼ cups	550 mL
Egg whites (large), room temperature	3	3
Cream of tartar	¼ tsp.	1 mL
Salt	⅛ tsp.	0.5 mL
Granulated sugar	⅓ cup	75 mL
Icing (confectioner's) sugar	½ cup	125 mL
Ground cinnamon	⅛ tsp.	0.5 mL
Semisweet chocolate baking square, finely grated	1 oz.	28 g
Finely crushed almonds, toasted	2 tbsp.	30 mL

Combine first 3 ingredients and press through fine meshed sieve into medium bowl. Stir in Vanilla Yogurt Cheese. Cover. Chill. Makes 2¼ cups (550 mL).

Beat egg whites, cream of tartar and salt in medium bowl until foamy. Slowly add granulated sugar until soft peaks form. Slowly add icing sugar, 1 tbsp. (15 mL) at a time, until meringue is glossy and stiff. Fold in cinnamon, chocolate and almonds. Cut parchment paper to fit baking sheets. Draw ten 4 inch (10 cm) ovals on one side. Turn paper over and tape to baking sheets. Pipe meringue onto oval using medium tip. Make thin base, slightly building up sides. Bake in 275°F (140°C) oven for 2½ hours, switching baking sheet positions at half-time. Leave in oven overnight, with door closed, to dry completely and cool. Fill centers of meringues with scant ¼ cup (60 mL) yogurt mixture just before serving. Makes 10 meringues.

NUTRITION INFORMATION 1 meringue: 151 Calories; 3.2 g Total Fat (1.7 g Sat., 6.2 mg Cholesterol); 133 mg Sodium; 7 g Protein; 25 g Carbohydrate; 1 g Dietary Fiber

CHOICES 1½ Milk; 1½ Sugar; 1 Fat & Oil

Pictured on page 54.

To grind instant coffee granules to a fine powder for above, crush with back of spoon in a small bowl.

French Pastry Dessert

A bit fussy to make, but it will get rave reviews. Must sit for 24 hours for soda crackers to soften into pastry layers.

All-purpose flour	3 tbsp.	50 mL
Cornstarch	3 tbsp.	50 mL
Salt	¼ tsp.	1 mL
Can of skim evaporated milk	13½ oz.	385 mL
Skim milk	1⅓ cups	325 mL
Sugar substitute (such as Sugar Twin)	⅓ cup	75 mL
Large egg, fork-beaten	1	1
Vanilla	2 tsp.	10 mL
Yellow food coloring (optional)		
Unsalted soda crackers	48	48
Light frozen whipped topping, thawed	4 cups	1 L
Can of sliced peaches in pear juice, drained (or Fresh Fruit Salad, page 60)	14 oz.	398 mL

Combine flour, cornstarch and salt in heavy-bottomed medium saucepan. Slowly add both milks. Whisk until smooth. Heat and stir on medium until boiling and thickened.

Whisk next 3 ingredients in small bowl. Add two spoonfuls of hot milk mixture to bowl. Mix well. Add to saucepan. Whisk together. Add food coloring to make custard color. Heat, stirring constantly, for 1 to 2 minutes until slightly thickened. Cover with plastic wrap directly on surface to prevent skin from forming. Cool to room temperature. Custard should still be runny, not set.

Line bottom of 9 x 9 inch (22 x 22 cm) pan with single layer of 16 crackers. Pour over or spoon on 1 cup (250 mL) custard in even layer. Spoon 1⅓ cups (325 mL) topping in small dabs over custard. Spread carefully. Repeat cracker, pudding and topping layers 2 more times, finishing with topping. Cover dessert with plastic wrap. Chill for at least 24 hours.

Arrange peaches on surface. Cuts into 9 pieces.

NUTRITION INFORMATION 1 piece: 259 Calories; 7.7 g Total Fat (5.3 g Sat., 26.3 mg Cholesterol); 347 mg Sodium; 8 g Protein; 39 g Carbohydrate; 1 g Dietary Fiber

CHOICES 1 Starch; 1 Fruit & Vegetable; 1 Milk; 1 Sugar; 1 Fat & Oil

If gelatin mixture becomes lumpy as it starts to set, warm it gently and stir until it is liquid again.

Cherry Chocolate Dessert

Fluffy and pretty topping on a fudgy base. So good you won't believe it's low fat!

Brownies, page 63		
Envelope of unflavored gelatin	¼ oz.	7 g
Reserved cherry syrup		
Package of sugar-free cherry-flavored gelatin (jelly powder)	3 oz.	85 g
Can of pitted cherries in syrup, drained, syrup reserved, chopped	14 oz.	398 mL
Non-fat spreadable cream cheese	8 oz.	225 g
Light liquid topping (such as Nutriwhip)	1 cup	250 mL
Chocolate curls, for garnish		

Bake brownies in greased 9 inch (22 cm) springform pan. Cool. Do not glaze.

Sprinkle unflavored gelatin over reserved syrup in small saucepan. Let stand for 5 minutes. Heat and stir on medium until boiling. Pour into large bowl.

Stir in jelly powder until dissolved. Stir in cherries. Whisk in cream cheese until well-blended. Chill for about 15 minutes, stirring 3 to 4 times, until syrupy and cherries stay suspended.

Beat topping in large bowl until stiff peaks form. Fold into cherry mixture. Spread on brownies only to edge. Chill for 4 to 5 hours until set.

Garnish with chocolate curls. Cuts into 12 pieces.

NUTRITION INFORMATION 1 piece: 224 Calories; 6.3 g Total Fat (1.4 g Sat., 0 mg Cholesterol); 59 mg Sodium; 5 g Protein; 39 g Carbohydrate; 3 g Dietary Fiber

CHOICES ½ Starch; 1 Fruit & Vegetable; 2 Sugar; ½ Protein; 1 Fat & Oil

Pictured on front cover and on page 53.

Fruit Crumble

Good fruity flavor with a crunchy topping. Serve with frozen vanilla yogurt.

Can of sliced peaches in pear juice	14 oz.	398 mL
Dried pitted prunes (about ⅔ cup, 150 mL)	15	15
Whole wheat flour	⅓ cup	75 mL
Quick-cooking rolled oats (not instant)	⅓ cup	75 mL
Brown sugar, packed	2 tbsp.	30 mL
Salt	¼ tsp.	1 mL
Margarine	2 tbsp.	30 mL

(continued on next page)

Pour peaches with juice into lightly greased 1 quart (1 L) shallow baking dish or 8 × 8 inch (20 × 20 cm) pan. Arrange prunes on peaches.

Combine next 4 ingredients in medium bowl. Cut in margarine until mixture is mealy and crumbly. Sprinkle evenly over fruit. Bake, uncovered, in 350°F (175°C) oven for 35 to 40 minutes until browned. Makes 2¾ cups (675 mL).

NUTRITION INFORMATION ½ cup (125 mL): 194 Calories; 4.9 g Total Fat (1.5 g Sat., 0 mg Cholesterol); 183 mg Sodium; 3 g Protein; 37 g Carbohydrate; 4 g Dietary Fiber

CHOICES 1 Starch; 2 Fruit & Vegetable; ½ Sugar; 1 Fat & Oil

Pineapple Nut Kuchen

This kuchen (KOO-ken) is a not-too-sweet dessert that is also great served at brunch.

All-purpose flour	½ cup	125 mL
Yellow cornmeal	½ cup	125 mL
Quick-cooking rolled oats (not instant)	⅓ cup	75 mL
Baking powder	1 tsp.	5 mL
Baking soda	⅛ tsp.	0.5 mL
Ground cinnamon	⅛ tsp.	0.5 mL
Non-fat plain yogurt	½ cup	125 mL
Large egg, fork-beaten	1	1
Brown sugar, packed	¼ cup	60 mL
Margarine, melted	2 tbsp.	30 mL
Can of pineapple tidbits, well-drained	14 oz.	398 mL
Chopped pecans	2 tbsp.	30 mL
Liquid honey, warmed	2 tbsp.	30 mL

Combine first 6 ingredients in medium bowl.

Beat next 4 ingredients in small bowl. Add to dry ingredients. Stir just until moistened. Turn into greased small quiche dish or 9 inch (22 cm) glass pie plate.

Scatter pineapple and pecans over top of batter. Press lightly with palm of hand. Drizzle with honey. Bake, uncovered, in 350°F (175°C) oven for 25 minutes until wooden pick inserted in center comes out clean. Serve warm. Cuts into 8 wedges.

NUTRITION INFORMATION 1 wedge: 188 Calories; 5.1 g Total Fat (0.9 g Sat., 27.2 mg Cholesterol); 79 mg Sodium; 4 g Protein; 32 g Carbohydrate; 2 g Dietary Fiber

CHOICES 1 Starch; ½ Fruit & Vegetable; 1 Sugar; 1 Fat & Oil

Pictured on page 53.

Chocolate Mousse

Melt-in-your-mouth creaminess. Use to fill phyllo cups or meringues or serve as a pudding dessert.

Cocoa	2 tbsp.	30 mL
Cornstarch	1 tbsp.	15 mL
All-purpose flour	1 tbsp.	15 mL
Salt	1/8 tsp.	0.5 mL
Can of skim evaporated milk	13 1/2 oz.	385 mL
Frozen egg product, thawed (see Note)	1/2 cup	125 mL
Envelope of unflavored gelatin	1/4 oz.	7 g
Cold water	1/4 cup	60 mL
Sugar substitute (such as Sugar Twin)	1/4 cup	60 mL
Vanilla	1 tsp.	5 mL
Egg whites (large)	3	3

Light frozen whipped topping, for garnish
Shaved chocolate, for garnish

Combine cocoa, cornstarch, flour and salt in medium saucepan. Slowly whisk in evaporated milk until smooth. Heat on medium, stirring frequently, until boiling and slightly thickened. Remove from heat.

Measure egg product into small bowl. Stir in two large spoonfuls of chocolate mixture. Slowly whisk back into chocolate mixture.

Combine gelatin and water in small dish. Let stand for 5 minutes. Whisk into chocolate mixture. Heat and stir on medium for 2 to 3 minutes until slightly thickened. Do not boil. Remove from heat.

Stir in sugar substitute and vanilla. Cover with plastic wrap directly on surface to prevent skin from forming. Cool for about 30 minutes until starting to set around the edges. Beat on high speed in large bowl for several minutes until thickened and creamy.

With clean beaters, beat egg whites in medium bowl until soft peaks form. Gently fold egg whites into chocolate mixture. Cover. Chill several hours or overnight until set.

Garnish with whipped topping and shaved chocolate. Makes 4 cups (1 L).

NUTRITION INFORMATION 1/2 cup (125 mL): 70 Calories; 0.3 g Total Fat (0.1 g Sat., 1.9 mg Cholesterol); 156 mg Sodium; 8 g Protein; 9 g Carbohydrate; 1 g Dietary Fiber

CHOICES 1 Milk; 1 Protein

Pictured on page 53 and on back cover.

Note: 4 tbsp. (50 mL) =1 large egg

Peach Packages

A perfect amount of peach filling is encased in layers of pastry.

Chopped fresh (or frozen, thawed) peaches	2 cups	500 mL
Lemon juice	1 tbsp.	15 mL
Brown sugar, packed	1 tbsp.	15 mL
Raisins	2 tbsp.	30 mL
Ground cinnamon	½ tsp.	2 mL
Ground ginger	¼ tsp.	1 mL
Minute tapioca	2 tsp.	10 mL
Fine dry whole wheat bread crumbs	2 tbsp.	30 mL
Brown sugar, packed	1½ tsp.	7 mL
Ground cinnamon	¼ tsp.	1 mL
Frozen phyllo pastry sheets, thawed	12	12
Granulated sugar (optional)	1 tsp.	5 mL
Ground cinnamon (optional)	¹⁄₁₆ tsp.	0.5 mL

Combine first 7 ingredients in medium bowl. Let stand for 10 minutes.

Mix bread crumbs and second amounts of brown sugar and cinnamon in small bowl.

Lay 1 sheet phyllo on flat surface. Sprinkle with ½ tbsp. (7 mL) bread crumb mixture. Cover with second sheet. Fold in half widthwise. Spoon ⅙ of peach mixture (generous ⅓ cup, 75 mL) about 2 inches (5 cm) from narrow end, leaving about 2 inches (5 cm) phyllo on either side. Roll edge over pastry. Tuck in sides and continue rolling until filling is completely enclosed. Place seam side down on lightly sprayed baking sheet. Repeat to make 5 more packages.

Spray packages with no-stick cooking spray. Lightly sprinkle with sugar and cinnamon. Bake in 375°F (190°C) oven for 20 minutes until golden brown. Makes 6 packages.

NUTRITION INFORMATION 1 package: 208 Calories; 1.2 g Total Fat (0.2 g Sat., trace Cholesterol); 290 mg Sodium; 5 g Protein; 46 g Carbohydrate; 2 g Dietary Fiber

CHOICES 2 Starch; 1 Fruit & Vegetable; ½ Sugar

APPLE CRANBERRY PACKAGES: Omit peaches. Add 2 medium apples, peeled and sliced, and ⅓ cup (75 mL) chopped dried cranberries.

To plump raisins or other dried fruit, cover with boiling water. Let stand for 1 minute. Drain.

Lemon Chiffon Filling

Fluffy, light and airy — all describe this fresh-tasting filling. Great for individual puddings or a pie. See below.

Envelopes of unflavored gelatin (¼ oz., 7 g, each)	2	2
Unsweetened pineapple juice	1 cup	250 mL
Liquid honey	1 tbsp.	15 mL
Salt, pinch		
Fresh lemon juice	3 tbsp.	50 mL
Grated lemon peel	1 tsp.	5 mL
Drops of yellow food coloring (optional)	3	3
Light frozen whipped topping	2 cups	500 mL
Lemon skim milk yogurt	1 cup	250 mL

Sprinkle gelatin over pineapple juice in medium saucepan. Let stand for 5 minutes. Heat and stir on medium until gelatin is dissolved. Stir in honey, salt, lemon juice, peel and food coloring. Chill, stirring several times, until syrupy.

Whip liquid topping according to package directions. Fold into gelatin mixture. Fold in yogurt. Pour into 8 individual dishes. Chill until set. Makes 4 cups (1 L).

NUTRITION INFORMATION ½ cup (125 mL): 97 Calories; 2.7 g Total Fat (2.5 g Sat., 0.6 mg Cholesterol); 30 mg Sodium; 3 g Protein; 15 g Carbohydrate; trace Dietary Fiber

CHOICES ½ Fruit & Vegetable; ½ Milk; ½ Sugar; ½ Fat & Oil

LEMON FRUIT PUDDING: Layer filling and fresh fruit in individual clear wine glasses or fruit nappies. Chill until set.

LEMON PIE: Pour filling into prepared Graham Bran Pie Crust, page 55. Chill until set.

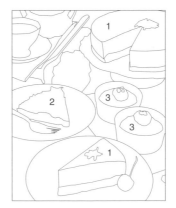

1. Cherry Chocolate Dessert, page 48
2. Pineapple Nut Kuchen, page 49
3. Chocolate Mousse, page 50

Graham Bran Pie Crust

Crisp, nutty flavor. Use Lemon Chiffon Filling, page 52, for a light, fluffy pie.

Graham cracker crumbs	1¼ cups	300 mL
All-bran cereal	½ cup	125 mL
Margarine, melted	1 tbsp.	15 mL
Non-fat vanilla (or plain) yogurt	2 tbsp.	30 mL
Orange (or apple) juice	1 tbsp.	15 mL
Ground cinnamon	¼ tsp.	1 mL
Ground nutmeg, sprinkle		

Blend or process graham crumbs and cereal until very finely ground. Empty into medium bowl.

Add remaining 5 ingredients. Mix until blended. Press into greased 9 inch (22 cm) pie plate. Bake in center of 325°F (160°C) oven for 8 to 10 minutes until set. Remove before too brown. Makes one 9 inch (22 cm) pie crust.

NUTRITION INFORMATION ⅛ crust: 95 Calories; 3.1 g Total Fat (0.7 g Sat., 0.1 mg Cholesterol); 179 mg Sodium; 2 g Protein; 17 g Carbohydrate; 2 g Dietary Fiber

CHOICES 1 Starch; ½ Fat & Oil

1. Brownies, page 63
2. Mocha Nut Meringues, page 46
3. Chocolate Éclair Dessert, page 62
4. Blueberry Layered Pudding, page 59

Piña Colada Pie

The cookie crust holds a silky textured filling with little pineapple bits.

OATMEAL COCONUT CRUST

All-purpose flour	**³/₄ cup**	**175 mL**
Quick-cooking rolled oats (not instant)	**¹/₃ cup**	**75 mL**
Flake coconut	**¹/₄ cup**	**60 mL**
Salt	**¹/₄ tsp.**	**1 mL**
Canola oil	**¹/₄ cup**	**60 mL**
Ice water	**3-4 tbsp.**	**50-60 mL**

FILLING

Can of crushed pineapple, drained and juice reserved	**14 oz.**	**398 mL**
Skim evaporated milk	**¹/₃ cup**	**75 mL**
Envelope of unflavored gelatin	**¹/₄ oz.**	**7 g**
Non-fat creamed cottage cheese	**³/₄ cup**	**175 mL**
Coconut flavoring	**1 tsp.**	**5 mL**
Granulated sugar (or sugar substitute, such as Sugar Twin, to equal)	**1 tbsp.**	**15 mL**
Reserved pineapple		
Envelope of dessert topping (not prepared)	**1¹/₂ oz.**	**42.5 g**
Reserved pineapple juice, chilled	**¹/₂ cup**	**125 mL**
Toasted flake coconut	**2 tbsp.**	**30 mL**

Oatmeal Coconut Crust: Combine first 4 ingredients in medium bowl. Drizzle on canola oil while mixing with fork.

Add water, 1 tbsp. (15 mL) at a time. Toss well with fork each time until dough forms ball. Roll between sheets of waxed paper to fit 9 inch (22 cm) pie plate. Remove waxed paper on one side. Turn into pie plate, waxed paper side up. Remove second sheet of waxed paper. Form shell and flute edge. Poke with fork in several places. Bake in 400°F (205°C) oven for 10 to 15 minutes until crust is golden brown. Cool.

Filling: Set aside pineapple. Chill ¹/₂ cup (125 mL) reserved juice. Combine remaining juice and evaporated milk in small saucepan. Sprinkle with gelatin. Let stand for 5 minutes. Heat and stir on medium just until gelatin is dissolved. Cool to room temperature.

Place cottage cheese, coconut flavoring and sugar in blender. Process, adding gelatin mixture gradually through lid, until smooth. Pour into large bowl. Fold in pineapple. Chill for about 15 minutes until just starting to thicken.

Beat topping and chilled juice in small bowl until stiff peaks form. Fold into cottage cheese mixture. Pour into cooled pie shell. Sprinkle with coconut. Chill until firm. Cuts into 8 wedges.

NUTRITION INFORMATION 1 wedge: 245 Calories; 11.4 g Total Fat (3.9 g Sat., 0.4 mg Cholesterol); 159 mg Sodium; 8 g Protein; 29 g Carbohydrate; 1 g Dietary Fiber

CHOICES 1 Starch; 1 Fruit & Vegetable; ¹/₂ Sugar; 1 Protein; 1¹/₂ Fat & Oil

Pumpkin Mousse In A Ginger Crust

Makes two pies for company. Delicious served frozen.

Low-fat gingersnap crumbs (see Tip, below)	**3 cups**	**750 mL**
Margarine, melted	**¹/₂ cup**	**125 mL**
Brown sugar, packed	**¹/₃ cup**	**75 mL**
Salt	**¹/₄ tsp.**	**1 mL**
Ground nutmeg	**¹/₄ tsp.**	**1 mL**
Ground ginger	**¹/₂ tsp.**	**2 mL**
Ground cinnamon	**¹/₂ tsp.**	**2 mL**
Envelopes of unflavored gelatin (¹/₄ oz., 7 g, each)	**2**	**2**
Skim evaporated milk	**³/₄ cup**	**175 mL**
Frozen egg product, thawed (see Note)	**¹/₂ cup**	**125 mL**
Can of pumpkin (without spices)	**14 oz.**	**398 mL**
Egg whites (large), room temperature	**3**	**3**
Granulated sugar	**¹/₄ cup**	**60 mL**

Combine gingersnap crumbs and margarine in medium bowl. Pack into bottom and up sides of two 9 inch (22 cm) pie plates. Bake in 350°F (175°C) oven for 8 to 10 minutes until firm. Cool.

Combine brown sugar, salt, nutmeg, ginger, cinnamon and gelatin in medium saucepan. Slowly stir in evaporated milk, egg product and pumpkin. Whisk together until smooth. Heat and stir on medium until thickened and gelatin is dissolved. Chill, stirring occasionally, until mixture mounds when dropped from spoon.

Beat egg whites in large clean bowl until soft peaks start to form. While beating, add granulated sugar, 1 tbsp. (15 mL) at a time, until stiff peaks form. Fold in pumpkin mixture. Divide filling between two crusts. Chill for several hours or overnight to set. Each pie cuts into 16 wedges.

NUTRITION INFORMATION 1 wedge: 224 Calories; 8.2 g Total Fat (3.7 g Sat., 16.6 mg Cholesterol); 306 mg Sodium; 5 g Protein; 33 g Carbohydrate; 1 g Dietary Fiber

CHOICES 1 Starch; ¹/₂ Fruit & Vegetable; ¹/₂ Sugar; 1 Fat & Oil

Note: 4 tbsp. (50 mL) =1 large egg

FROZEN PUMPKIN DESSERT: Reserve ¹/₂ cup (125 mL) gingersnap crumbs. Pack remainder in bottom and up sides of 10 inch (25 cm) springform pan or bottom of 9 x 13 inch (22 x 33 cm) pan. Pour in filling. Sprinkle with reserved crumbs. Chill to set. Freeze.

To make gingersnap crumbs, process whole cookies in food processor or blender until desired consistency.

Creamy Rice Pudding

Very creamy with minimal fat in the 2% milk. Using skim milk will produce a curdled pudding.

Can of skim evaporated milk	13½ oz.	385 mL
2% milk	2 cups	500 mL
Cooked white rice	2 cups	500 mL
Liquid (or creamed) honey	¼ cup	60 mL
Ground cinnamon	¼ tsp.	1 mL
Salt	¼ tsp.	1 mL
Light (or sultana) raisins	⅓ cup	75 mL
Frozen egg product, thawed (see Note)	½ cup	125 mL
Vanilla	2 tsp.	10 mL

Combine first 7 ingredients in large uncovered pot. Bring to a boil. Reduce heat. Simmer, uncovered, for 15 minutes, stirring frequently.

Measure egg product into small bowl. Add ½ cup (125 mL) hot mixture to eggs. Mix well. Stir into saucepan. Heat, stirring constantly, until thickened.

Remove from heat. Stir in vanilla. Cover with plastic wrap directly on surface to prevent skin from forming. Serve warm or cooled to room temperature. Makes 5¼ cups (1.3 L).

NUTRITION INFORMATION ½ cup (125 mL): 158 Calories; 1.2 g Total Fat (0.7 g Sat., 5.1 mg Cholesterol); 160 mg Sodium; 7 g Protein; 30 g Carbohydrate; 1 g Dietary Fiber

CHOICES 1 Starch; 1 Fruit & Vegetable; 1 Milk

Note: 4 tbsp. (50 mL) =1 large egg

Apricot Almond Pudding

A nice change from regular rice pudding. Serve warm or cold.

2% evaporated milk	1 cup	250 mL
Skim milk	2 cups	500 mL
Pearl (or arborio) rice	½ cup	125 mL
Salt	¼ tsp.	1 mL
Ground cinnamon	¼ tsp.	1 mL
Finely chopped dried apricots	⅓ cup	75 mL
Grated lemon zest (optional)	1 tsp.	5 mL
Sugar substitute (such as Sugar Twin)	1 tbsp.	15 mL
Almond flavoring	¼ tsp.	1 mL
Toasted crushed almonds (optional)	1 tbsp.	15 mL

Combine first 6 ingredients in top of double boiler. Heat over boiling water for about 45 minutes, stirring occasionally, until thickened and creamy.

(continued on next page)

Stir in lemon zest, sugar substitute and flavoring. Sprinkle with almonds. Makes 3 cups (750 mL).

NUTRITION INFORMATION ½ cup (125 mL): 152 Calories; 1.2 g Total Fat (0.7 g Sat., 5 mg Cholesterol); 208 mg Sodium; 8 g Protein; 28 g Carbohydrate; 1 g Dietary Fiber

CHOICES 1 Starch; ½ Fruit & Vegetable; 1½ Milk

RAISIN PUDDING: Omit apricots and almond flavoring. Add ⅓ cup (75 mL) raisins and ¼ tsp. (1 mL) vanilla. Sprinkle with cinnamon.

Blueberry Layered Pudding
Frozen cheesecake in a bowl.

Envelope of unflavored gelatin	¼ oz.	7 g
Cold water	¼ cup	60 mL
Non-fat spreadable cream cheese	8 oz.	225 g
Icing (confectioner's) sugar (omit if using regular pie filling)	2 tbsp.	30 mL
Non-fat lemon yogurt	26.8 oz.	750 g
Graham cracker crumbs	⅔ cup	150 mL
Can of calorie-reduced (or regular) blueberry pie filling	19 oz.	540 mL
Light frozen whipped topping, thawed, for garnish	1 cup	250 mL
Freshly grated lemon peel, for garnish		
Fresh blueberries, for garnish		

Stir gelatin into cold water in small saucepan. Let stand for 5 minutes. Heat and stir on low until liquid and gelatin is dissolved. Cool to warm room temperature but still liquid.

Beat cream cheese and icing sugar until smooth. Beat in gelatin and yogurt on very low speed until just mixed. Chill for 1 hour.

Place ⅓ of yogurt mixture in shallow 7 cup (1.75 L) clear glass bowl. Sprinkle with ⅓ cup (75 mL) graham crumbs. Spoon ½ of pie filling evenly over crumbs. Repeat layers, ending with final ⅓ of yogurt mixture. Swirl with spatula to create marble effect. Freeze for at least 4 hours until firm.

Garnish with whipped topping, grated lemon peel and fresh blueberries. Serves 8.

NUTRITION INFORMATION 1 serving: 198 Calories; 1.3 g Total Fat (0.3 g Sat., 2 mg Cholesterol); 132 mg Sodium; 8 g Protein; 40 g Carbohydrate; 1 g Dietary Fiber

CHOICES 1 Starch; 1 Fruit & Vegetable; 1½ Milk; 1 Sugar

FROZEN BLUEBERRY DESSERT: Assemble pudding layers as above in a freezer-safe bowl or pan. Swirl with spatula to create marble effect. Freeze for at least 4 hours until firm. Scoop to serve.

Pictured on page 54.

Fresh Fruit Salad

Serve by itself or over Lemon Cheesecake, page 45. Has a lovely sauce that forms while marinating in the refrigerator.

Sliced fresh strawberries	1 cup	250 mL
Diced ripe cantaloupe	1 cup	250 mL
Medium oranges, peeled, halved and thinly sliced	2	2
Ripe kiwifruit, peeled and diced	2	2
Sugar-free lemon-lime soft drink	¾ cup	175 mL
Medium banana, diced	1	1

Combine first 4 ingredients in medium bowl. Pour soft drink over top. Toss lightly. Cover. Chill for 1 hour to blend flavors.

Mix in banana. Makes 3 cups (750 mL).

NUTRITION INFORMATION ½ cup (125 mL): 66 Calories; 0.4 g Total Fat (trace Sat., 0 mg Cholesterol); 6 mg Sodium; 1 g Protein; 16 g Carbohydrate; 3 g Dietary Fiber

CHOICES 1½ Fruit & Vegetable

Strawberry Banana Frozen Yogurt

Try customizing the flavor by using different fruit.

Ripe medium banana	1	1
Whole fresh strawberries (5 large or 10 medium)	6 oz.	170 g
Non-fat vanilla yogurt	1 cup	250 mL
Lemon juice	1 tsp.	5 mL
Liquid honey	1½ tsp.	7 mL
Vanilla	½ tsp.	2 mL
Light frozen whipped topping, thawed	1 cup	250 mL

Cut banana into 1 inch (2.5 cm) chunks. Arrange with strawberries in single layer on baking sheet. Freeze for about 2 hours until hard.

Process frozen fruit with next 4 ingredients in food processor until slushy and smooth.

Fold in whipped topping. Empty into freezer container. Freeze for at least 3 hours. Stir well every half hour for the first 1½ hours. Makes 3½ cups (875 mL).

NUTRITION INFORMATION ½ cup (125 mL): 73 Calories; 1.7 g Total Fat (1.5 g Sat., 0.7 mg Cholesterol); 30 mg Sodium; 2 g Protein; 13 g Carbohydrate; 1 g Dietary Fiber

CHOICES ½ Fruit & Vegetable; ½ Milk; ½ Sugar

Ginger Lime Dip

A delightfully fresh taste to dip fresh fruit in.

Yogurt Cheese, page 75	¹/₂ cup	125 mL
Liquid honey	1 tbsp.	15 mL
Freshly squeezed lime juice	1 tbsp.	15 mL
Grated lime peel	¹/₄ tsp.	1 mL
Light frozen whipped topping, thawed	¹/₂ cup	125 mL
Ground ginger	¹/₄ tsp.	1 mL

Combine all 6 ingredients in small dish. Whisk until blended. Makes ³/₄ cup (175 mL).

NUTRITION INFORMATION 1 tbsp. (15 mL): 26 Calories; 0.8 g Total Fat (0.6 g Sat., 1.2 mg Cholesterol); 15 mg Sodium; 1 g Protein; 4 g Carbohydrate; trace Dietary Fiber

CHOICES ¹/₂ Milk

Milk Chocolate Sauce

Great served on a scoop of frozen vanilla yogurt.

Cocoa	2 tbsp.	30 mL
Vanilla custard powder	2 tbsp.	30 mL
Granulated sugar	2 tbsp.	30 mL
Can of skim evaporated milk	13¹/₂ oz.	385 mL
Margarine	1 tbsp.	15 mL
Vanilla	2 tsp.	10 mL

Combine cocoa, custard powder and sugar in small saucepan. Slowly whisk in evaporated milk until smooth. Add margarine. Heat and stir on medium until boiling and slightly thickened. Remove from heat.

Stir in vanilla. Makes 1¹/₂ cups (375 mL).

NUTRITION INFORMATION 2 tbsp. (30 mL): 55 Calories; 1.1 g Total Fat (0.3 g Sat., 1.2 mg Cholesterol); 57 mg Sodium; 3 g Protein; 9 g Carbohydrate; trace Dietary Fiber

CHOICES ¹/₂ Milk; ¹/₂ Sugar

To prevent milk from scorching, cook sauce in top pan of double boiler over boiling water. Or heat mixture in microwave on medium-high (80%), stirring frequently, until boiling and slightly thickened.

Chocolate Éclair Dessert

Amazing how the layers soften overnight into a cake-like texture. Great creamy chocolate flavor.

Cocoa	⅓ cup	75 mL
Cornstarch	2 tbsp.	30 mL
All-purpose flour	2 tbsp.	30 mL
Granulated sugar	½ cup	125 mL
Salt	⅛ tsp.	0.5 mL
Ground cinnamon	⅛ tsp.	0.5 mL
Skim milk	1 cup	250 mL
Can of skim evaporated milk	13½ oz.	385 mL
Frozen egg product, thawed (see Note)	½ cup	125 mL
Vanilla	1 tsp.	5 mL
Light liquid topping (such as Nutriwhip)	1 cup	250 mL
Cocoa, sifted	1 tbsp.	15 mL
Whole graham crackers	28	28
Cocoa, sifted, for garnish	1 tsp.	5 mL

Combine first amount of cocoa, cornstarch, flour, sugar, salt and cinnamon in medium saucepan. Slowly whisk in both milks until smooth. Heat and stir on medium until boiling and thickened. Remove from heat.

Add two large spoonfuls of hot pudding to egg product in small bowl. Mix well. Whisk into cocoa mixture until smooth. Heat for 2 minutes. Stir in vanilla. Cover with plastic wrap directly on the surface to prevent skin from forming. Let stand until cooled to room temperature.

Beat topping with second amount of cocoa in medium bowl until stiff.

Arrange ½ of graham crackers in single layer in 9 x 9 inch (22 x 22 cm) pan. Cut to fit if necessary. Whisk pudding to make smooth. Spread ½ of pudding mixture on crackers and spread evenly. Spread ½ of whipped topping mixture on pudding. Cover with single layer of remaining crackers, remaining pudding and topping. Cover with plastic wrap for 24 hours to allow crackers to soften completely.

Just before serving, sift cocoa over top. For a more decorative look, place doily over top of dessert, then sift with cocoa. Carefully lift and remove doily and excess cocoa. Cuts into 16 pieces.

NUTRITION INFORMATION 1 piece: 126 Calories; 2.1 g Total Fat (1 g Sat., 1.2 mg Cholesterol); 158 mg Sodium; 5 g Protein; 24 g Carbohydrate; 1 g Dietary Fiber

CHOICES 1 Starch; ½ Milk; ½ Sugar; ½ Fat & Oil

Pictured on page 54.

Note: 4 tbsp. (50 mL) =1 large egg

Brownies

These are a very good substitute for high-fat brownies. They are moist and rich. High in sugar so cut them small, and only indulge when you must have a sweet chocolate treat.

Frozen egg product, thawed (see Note)	**¹/₂ cup**	**125 mL**
Canola oil	**¹/₄ cup**	**60 mL**
Jar of strained prunes (baby food)	**4¹/₂ oz.**	**128 mL**
Vanilla	**2 tsp.**	**10 mL**
Brown sugar, packed	**¹/₂ cup**	**125 mL**
Granulated sugar	**¹/₂ cup**	**125 mL**
Cocoa	**¹/₂ cup**	**125 mL**
All-purpose flour	**²/₃ cup**	**150 mL**
Baking powder	**¹/₂ tsp.**	**2 mL**
Salt	**¹/₈ tsp.**	**0.5 mL**
GLAZE (optional)		
Cocoa	**1 tbsp.**	**15 mL**
Icing (confectioner's) sugar	**¹/₂ cup**	**125 mL**
Hot water	**1 tbsp.**	**15 mL**

Beat egg product, canola oil, prunes and vanilla until smooth. Beat in both sugars and cocoa. Beat in flour, baking powder and salt until smooth. Pour into greased 8 × 8 inch (20 × 20 cm) baking pan. Bake in 325°F (160°C) oven for 30 to 35 minutes just until center is set. Do not overcook.

Glaze: Combine all 3 ingredients in small bowl until smooth. Drizzle over warm brownies. Cool. Cuts into 25 squares.

NUTRITION INFORMATION 1 square: 78 Calories; 2.6 g Total Fat (0.3 g Sat., 0 mg Cholesterol); 26 mg Sodium; 1 g Protein; 14 g Carbohydrate; 1 g Dietary Fiber

CHOICES ¹/₂ Fruit & Vegetable; 1 Sugar; ¹/₂ Fat & Oil

Pictured on page 54.

Note: 4 tbsp. (50 mL) = 1 large egg

To prevent overbaking brownies, watch the edges for signs of pulling away from the pan. At that point, if a wooden pick inserted in the center comes out clean but moist, it is done.

Rainbow Fruit Pizza

So pretty, so delicious and so refreshing. Uses Tangy Lemon Spread, page 65.

CRUST		
All-purpose flour	¾ cup	175 mL
Quick-cooking rolled oats (not instant)	½ cup	125 mL
Brown sugar, packed	1 tbsp.	15 mL
Salt	⅛ tsp.	0.5 mL
Cold hard margarine, cut into 6 pieces	¼ cup	60 mL
Ice water	3 tbsp.	50 mL
Tangy Lemon Spread, page 65	1 cup	250 mL
Fresh (or frozen, thawed) blueberries	1 cup	250 mL
Sliced fresh strawberries	1 cup	250 mL
Small kiwifruit, peeled and sliced	2	2
Envelope of unflavored gelatin	¼ oz.	7 g
Unsweetened fruit juice	⅓ cup	75 mL
Liquid honey (optional)	2 tsp.	10 mL

Crust: Process first 4 ingredients in food processor or blender until oats are powdery. Add margarine. Pulse with on/off motion until crumbly.

Drizzle water, 1 tbsp. (15 mL) at a time, over dry ingredients. Pulse 4 to 5 times after each addition. Add enough water to make a ball. Roll out dough to 10 inch (25 cm) circle. Place on lightly greased baking sheet. Roll edge, making fluted design. Poke all over with fork. Chill. Bake in 450°F (230°C) oven for 12 to 15 minutes until golden brown. Cool on wire rack.

Spread crust with Tangy Lemon Spread. Arrange fruit in single layer on crust.

Soften gelatin in juice in small saucepan for 1 minute. Heat and stir on low until dissolved. Stir in honey. Cool to room temperature. Brush liberally on fruit. Chill well. Cuts into 10 wedges.

NUTRITION INFORMATION 1 wedge: 153 Calories; 5.5 g Total Fat (1.1 g Sat., 0.3 mg Cholesterol); 107 mg Sodium; 4 g Protein; 23 g Carbohydrate; 2 g Dietary Fiber

CHOICES 1 Starch; 1 Fruit & Vegetable; 1 Fat & Oil

Pictured on back cover.

Tangy Lemon Spread

Delicious on muffins and as the base for Rainbow Fruit Pizza, page 64. Try the variation — it makes a great fresh fruit dip.

Cornstarch	2 tbsp.	30 mL
Granulated sugar	1/4 cup	60 mL
Water	1/2 cup	125 mL
Lemon juice (fresh is best)	3 tbsp.	50 mL
Freshly grated lemon peel (optional)	1/4 tsp.	1 mL
Drops of yellow food coloring (optional)	2	2
Plain skim milk yogurt	1 cup	250 mL

Combine cornstarch and sugar in small saucepan. Add water. Heat and stir on medium until boiling and thickened.

Stir in lemon juice, peel and food coloring. Let cool.

Stir in yogurt. Chill. Makes 1²/₃ cups (400 mL).

NUTRITION INFORMATION 1 tbsp. (15 mL): 15 Calories; trace Total Fat (trace Sat., 0.2 mg Cholesterol); 7 mg Sodium; trace Protein; 3 g Carbohydrate; trace Dietary Fiber

CHOICES 1/2 Fruit & Vegetable

TANGY LEMON DIP: Fold in 1 cup (250 mL) light frozen whipped topping, thawed, for a fluffy, fresh fruit dip.

Sour Fruit Pops

Tart flavor will remind you of sour candies! A refreshing frozen treat for hot summer days or birthday parties.

Chopped fresh rhubarb	1 1/2 cups	375 mL
Water	2/3 cup	150 mL
Package of regular (or sugar-free) strawberry-flavored gelatin (jelly powder)	3 oz.	85 g
Chopped fresh strawberries	1 1/2 cups	375 mL
Non-fat vanilla yogurt	1/2 cup	125 mL

Cook rhubarb in water in small saucepan for 10 minutes, stirring frequently, until softened. Stir in jelly powder until dissolved. Pour into blender.

Add strawberries and yogurt. Process until smooth. Pour 1/4 cup (60 mL) into each popsicle form and insert handles. Freeze until solid. Makes 12 popsicles.

NUTRITION INFORMATION 1 popsicle: 41 Calories; 0.1 g Total Fat (trace Sat., 0.2 mg Cholesterol); 29 mg Sodium; 1 g Protein; 9 g Carbohydrate; 1 g Dietary Fiber

CHOICES 1 Fruit & Vegetable

Variation: Pour 1/2 cup (125 mL) of mixture into 6 small waxed paper cups. Insert wooden stick when partially frozen.

• DESSERTS •

Lunch

Whether you're brown bagging it or sitting down at the kitchen table, lunch can be imaginative and appetizing. Taking a bag lunch to work or school doesn't mean your only lunch options are fat and sodium-filled processed meats and chips or sugar-laden chocolate bars. These nutritious recipes are sure to draw envious glances from fellow students or colleagues.

Individual Pizzas

Pizzas that taste great and are quick to make using staples you have in your home. Don't limit yourself to these toppings. Try any combination that appeals to you.

Pizza sauce	1 tbsp.	15 mL
Pita bread (7-8 inch, 18-20 cm, size)	1	1
Grated part-skim mozzarella cheese	1/3 cup	75 mL
VEGETARIAN TOPPING		
Garlic powder	1/8 tsp.	0.5 mL
Small roma (plum) tomato, seeded and diced (about 1/3 cup, 75 mL)	1	1
Finely slivered red onion	2 tbsp.	30 mL
Medium fresh mushrooms, finely diced (about 2 tbsp., 30 mL)	2	2
Dried sweet basil, crushed	1/8 tsp.	0.5 mL
Grated light Parmesan cheese	1 tsp.	5 mL
HAM AND MUSHROOM TOPPING		
Fat-free ham slice (3/4 oz., 21 g), diced	1	1
Medium fresh mushrooms (about 1/3 cup, 75 mL), sliced	3	3
Finely diced green pepper	1 tbsp.	15 mL
Grated light Parmesan cheese	1 tsp.	5 mL
Freshly ground pepper, sprinkle		

Spread sauce on pita to edges. Sprinkle cheese evenly over sauce.

Topping (Vegetarian or Ham And Mushroom): Cover with toppings in order given. Place on baking sheet. Bake, uncovered, in 400°F (205°C) oven on center rack for 10 minutes until crispy and browned. Makes 1 pizza.

NUTRITION INFORMATION 1 vegetarian pizza: 248 Calories; 4 g Total Fat (1.9 g Sat., 9.3 mg Cholesterol); 405 mg Sodium; 12 g Protein; 42 g Carbohydrate; 2 g Dietary Fiber

1 ham and mushroom pizza: 243 Calories; 3.8 g Total Fat (1.8 g Sat., 9.3 mg Cholesterol); 660 mg Sodium; 14 g Protein; 38 g Carbohydrate; 1 g Dietary Fiber

CHOICES 1 vegetarian pizza: 2 Starch; 1 Fruit & Vegetable; 1 Protein

1 ham and mushroom pizza: 2 Starch; 1/2 Fruit & Vegetable; 1 Protein

Pictured on page 71.

• LUNCH •

Italian Stuffed Peppers

Wild rice and chicken in fleshy, sweet peppers. Yum!

Package of long grain and wild rice mix	6½ oz.	180 g
Chopped onion	½ cup	125 mL
Garlic clove, minced	1	1
Chopped fresh mushrooms	1½ cups	375 mL
Grated carrot	¼ cup	60 mL
Canola oil	1 tsp.	5 mL
Ground chicken breast	10 oz.	284 mL
Can of tomato sauce	7½ oz.	213 mL
Chopped fresh sweet basil (or 1 tsp., 5 mL, dried)	2 tbsp.	30 mL
Chopped fresh oregano leaves (or ½ tsp., 2 mL, dried)	2 tbsp.	30 mL
Salt	¼ tsp.	1 mL
Pepper	⅛ tsp.	0.5 mL
Medium green peppers, halved lengthwise	4	4
Water	¼ cup	60 mL
Grated part-skim mozzarella cheese	½ cup	125 mL

Prepare rice as directed on package but without margarine.

Sauté onion, garlic, mushrooms and carrot in canola oil until soft. Add ground chicken. Scramble-fry until chicken is no longer pink.

Add cooked rice, tomato sauce, basil, oregano, salt and pepper.

Stuff each pepper half with ¾ cup (175 mL) filling. Place in 9 x 13 inch (22 x 33 cm) pan. Pour water into pan. Cover with foil. Bake in 350°F (175°C) oven for 40 minutes until peppers are tender-crisp.

Remove foil. Top each pepper with 1 tbsp. (15 mL) mozzarella cheese. Bake for 5 minutes until cheese is melted. Makes 8 stuffed peppers.

NUTRITION INFORMATION 1 stuffed pepper: 176 Calories; 2.7 g Total Fat (1 g Sat., 25.1 mg Cholesterol); 477 mg Sodium; 13 g Protein; 25 g Carbohydrate; 2 g Dietary Fiber

CHOICES 1 Starch; 1 Fruit & Vegetable; 1½ Protein

Wild rice is the seed of a wild, aquatic grass. To save money, make your own mix of wild and long grain rice by combining 20% wild rice with 80% long grain rice.

Parkerhouse Pockets

Golden, cheese-filled rolls delicious with salad or as part of a brunch.

Part-skim ricotta cheese	8 oz.	250 g
Green onions, with tops, finely sliced	4	4
Small potato, peeled, cooked and mashed	1	1
Skim milk	1¼ cups	300 mL
Granulated sugar	⅓ cup	75 mL
Canola oil	¼ cup	60 mL
Salt	¾ tsp.	4 mL
Whole wheat flour	2 cups	500 mL
Package of instant yeast (or 2¼ tsp., 11 mL, bulk)	¼ oz.	8 g
Egg white (large), fork-beaten	1	1
All-purpose flour	2-2½ cups	500-625 mL

Combine cream cheese and green onion in small bowl. Set aside.

Combine next 5 ingredients in small saucepan. Heat and stir on medium until sugar is dissolved. Cool to very warm but not hot.

Combine whole wheat flour and yeast in large bowl. Stir in wet ingredients until thick batter consistency. Add egg white. Mix well. Add all-purpose flour, ½ cup (125 mL) at a time, until soft dough is formed. Turn out and knead on floured surface for about 10 minutes until smooth and elastic. Cover. Let rest 15 minutes in oven with light on and door closed. Cut dough in half. Roll one portion out on lightly floured surface to scant ½ inch (12 mm) thickness. Cut with three inch (7 cm) cutter. Fill middle with 1 tsp. (5 mL) cheese mixture. Fold over and pinch side like perogy. Repeat with remaining dough. Arrange pockets on 2 large greased baking sheets. Cover. Let rise in oven with light on and door closed for 40 minutes until doubled in size. Bake in 350°F (175°C) oven for 20 to 25 minutes until golden brown. Makes 24 pockets.

NUTRITION INFORMATION 1 pocket: 144 Calories; 3.6 g Total Fat (0.8 g Sat., 3.5 mg Cholesterol); 108 mg Sodium; 5 g Protein; 24 g Carbohydrate; 2 g Dietary Fiber

CHOICES 1 Starch; 1 Milk; ½ Fat & Oil

Pictured on page 71.

tip Sugar in breads acts as food for the yeast to help produce carbon dioxide, which makes the dough rise. Sugar is also used for flavor and helps the crust brown. Honey or molasses may also be used in the recipe for the same effects.

Pizza Pockets

Perfect for eating with your hands. Freeze and reheat for lunches!

Lean ground chicken (or beef or pork)	8 oz.	225 g
Chopped onion	1 cup	250 mL
Garlic clove, minced	1	1
Grated zucchini, with peel	1 cup	250 mL
Can of regular (or low-sodium) tomato sauce	7½ oz.	213 mL
Dried whole oregano	½ tsp.	2 mL
Dried sweet basil	1 tsp.	5 mL
Freshly ground pepper	⅛ tsp.	0.5 mL
Dried crushed chilies	⅛ tsp.	0.5 mL
Grated part-skim mozzarella cheese	¾ cup	175 mL
Grated light Parmesan cheese	2 tbsp.	30 mL
Whole wheat flour	⅔ cup	150 mL
All-purpose flour	1 cup	250 mL
Baking powder	4 tsp.	20 mL
Salt	½ tsp.	2 mL
Canola oil	3 tbsp.	50 mL
Skim milk	¾ cup	175 mL
All-purpose flour	⅓ cup	75 mL
Skim milk	¼ cup	60 mL

Sauté chicken, onion, garlic and zucchini in large non-stick frying pan until no pink remains in chicken and liquid is evaporated.

Stir in next 5 ingredients. Heat, uncovered, for 10 minutes on low, stirring occasionally, until thickened. Remove from heat. Let stand to cool slightly. Stir in both cheeses.

Combine whole wheat flour, first amount of all-purpose flour, baking powder and salt in medium bowl. Make a well in center.

Combine canola oil and first amount of milk in small bowl. Add, all at once, to dry ingredients. Stir with fork just until moistened.

Turn out and gently knead dough on floured surface, using second amount of all-purpose flour, about 8 to 10 times. Divide dough into 8 portions. Roll each out to 6 inch (15 cm) circle. Place ⅓ cup (75 mL) filling to one side of center. Moisten edge of dough with some of second amount of milk. Bring unfilled side of dough over filling and press edges together with fork tines to seal well. Cut 3 or 4 slits in top with tip of sharp knife. Place on greased baking sheet. Brush with remaining milk. Bake in 400°F (205°C) oven for 13 to15 minutes until golden brown. Makes 8 pockets.

NUTRITION INFORMATION 1 pocket: 263 Calories; 8.2 g Total Fat (1.9 g Sat., 24.2 mg Cholesterol); 464 mg Sodium; 16 g Protein; 32 g Carbohydrate; 3 g Dietary Fiber

CHOICES 2 Starch; ½ Fruit & Vegetable; 1½ Protein; 1 Fat & Oil

Chicken In Peppers

Can be used as an appetizer or a brunch/lunch offering.

Lean ground chicken	8 oz.	225 g
Thinly sliced green onion	2 tbsp.	30 mL
Finely chopped celery	2 tbsp.	30 mL
Garlic clove, minced	1	1
Cornstarch	2 tsp.	10 mL
Ground ginger	½ tsp.	2 mL
Sherry (or alcohol-free sherry)	2 tsp.	10 mL
Black Bean Sauce, page 86 (or commercial)	2 tbsp.	30 mL
Large peppers (your choice of color, or mixed)	2	2
Toasted sesame seeds	1 tbsp.	15 mL

Combine first 8 ingredients in small bowl.

Cut peppers in ½ crosswise and then quarter each half to make little cups. Remove seeds. Pack about 1½ tsp. (7 mL) chicken mixture in each pepper piece. Place on rack over boiling water or in bamboo steamer. Steam for 8 to 10 minutes until chicken is cooked and peppers are bright green and tender-crisp.

Sprinkle with sesame seeds. Makes 16 pieces.

NUTRITION INFORMATION 1 piece: 29 Calories; 0.5 g Total Fat (0.1 g Sat., 8.2 mg Cholesterol); 33 mg Sodium; 4 g Protein; 2 g Carbohydrate; trace Dietary Fiber

CHOICES ½ Protein; Extra

Pictured on front cover.

1. Lemonberry Smoothie, page 25
2. Individual Pizzas, page 66
3. Parkerhouse Pockets, page 68
4. Tuna Toast, page 73

Tuna Toast

Deliciously different for lunch or brunch.

Whole wheat bread slices	**4**	**4**
Margarine (optional)	**4 tsp.**	**20 mL**
Can of white tuna, packed in water, drained and flaked	**6 oz.**	**170 g**
Fresh asparagus, cooked (or 1 can, 12 oz., 341 mL, drained)	**8 oz.**	**225 g**
Egg whites (large)	**2**	**2**
Light salad dressing	**¼ cup**	**60 mL**
Chili sauce	**1 tbsp.**	**15 mL**
Paprika, sprinkle		

Toast bread slices. Spread one side of each with 1 tsp. (5 mL) margarine if desired.

Spread ¼ of tuna on buttered side of each slice of toast. Top with asparagus. Place on baking sheet.

Beat egg whites in medium bowl until very stiff. Fold in dressing and chili sauce. Divide and spread egg white mixture right to edges over tuna and asparagus. Sprinkle with paprika. Bake in 400°F (205°C) oven on center rack for 8 minutes until meringue topping is golden. Cut diagonally into 4 pieces.

NUTRITION INFORMATION 1 piece: 190 Calories; 5.8 g Total Fat (0.6 g Sat., 17 mg Cholesterol); 506 mg Sodium; 16 g Protein; 20 g Carbohydrate; 3 g Dietary Fiber

CHOICES 1 Starch; ½ Fruit & Vegetable; 2 Protein

Variation: Omit asparagus. Slice medium tomato ½ inch (12 mm). Arrange on tuna.

Pictured on page 71.

1. Pad Thai, page 110
2. Fruit-Stuffed Pork Loin, page 112
3. Stuffed Tomatoes, page 139
4. Lentil Rice, page 134
5. Grilled Hoisin Flank Steak, page 80

Tuna Salad Pitas

The Yogurt Cheese offers such a fresh-tasting change from the usual mayonnaise.

Can of white tuna, packed in water, well-drained	4 oz.	113 g
Diced English cucumber, with peel	¼ cup	60 mL
Medium roma (plum) tomato, seeded and diced	1	1
Dill weed	¼ tsp.	1 mL
Celery salt	⅛ tsp.	0.5 mL
Yogurt Cheese, page 75	½ cup	125 mL
Small pita breads (3 inch, 7.5 cm, size)	6	6

Break up tuna with fork in medium bowl. Toss with cucumber, tomato, dill weed and celery salt. Stir in Yogurt Cheese.

Tear open pitas on one side. Fill with ¼ cup (60 mL) tuna mixture. Makes 6 pitas.

NUTRITION INFORMATION 1 pita: 95 Calories; 1.3 g Total Fat (0.5 g Sat., 10 mg Cholesterol); 179 mg Sodium; 9 g Protein; 12 g Carbohydrate; trace Dietary Fiber

CHOICES 1 Starch; 1 Protein

Spicy Refried Beans

Spread on flour tortillas and heat in the microwave for a delicious bean burrito.

Chopped onion	½ cup	125 mL
Garlic clove, minced	1	1
Water	1 tbsp.	15 mL
Brown sugar, packed	1 tsp.	5 mL
Canola oil	1 tsp.	5 mL
Chili powder	½ tsp.	2 mL
Cayenne pepper	⅛ tsp.	0.5 mL
Can of pinto beans, with liquid	14 oz.	398 mL
Apple cider vinegar	2 tsp.	10 mL
Salt	⅛ tsp.	0.5 mL

Sauté onion, garlic, water and brown sugar in canola oil in non-stick frying pan on medium-low for about 15 minutes until onion is golden and very soft. Stir in chili powder and cayenne. Sauté for 1 to 2 minutes.

Drain beans, reserving ¼ cup (60 mL) liquid. Process beans, reserved liquid, vinegar and salt in food processor or blender until mushy. Add to onion mixture. Heat on medium-low for 2 to 3 minutes until mixture is dry and paste-like. Makes 1⅓ cups (325 mL).

NUTRITION INFORMATION ¼ cup (60 mL): 79 Calories; 1.2 g Total Fat (0.1 g Sat., 0 mg Cholesterol); 388 mg Sodium; 4 g Protein; 14 g Carbohydrate; trace Dietary Fiber

CHOICES 1 Starch

Yogurt Cheese

Use this thick yogurt for spreads, dips and desserts. Use in Tuna Salad Pitas, page 74, or Mocha Nut Meringues, page 46.

Low-fat plain yogurt, without gelatin	28 oz.	907 g

Line plastic strainer with a double thickness of cheesecloth. Place over deep bowl. Spoon in yogurt. Cover loosely with plastic wrap. Drain in refrigerator for 24 hours, discarding whey in bowl several times. Remove to sealable container. Cover. Store in refrigerator until expiry date on yogurt container. Makes 2 cups (500 mL).

NUTRITION INFORMATION ¼ cup (60 mL): 71 Calories; 1.8 g Total Fat (1.1 g Sat., 6.9 mg Cholesterol); 79 mg Sodium; 6 g Protein; 8 g Carbohydrate; 0 g Dietary Fiber

CHOICES 1½ Milk

VANILLA YOGURT CHEESE: Omit low-fat plain yogurt. Use 4 cups (1 L) of low-fat vanilla yogurt. Makes 2⅛ cups (530 mL).

Beef Coleslaw Pitas

Dill pickles give these a bit of tang. Good and crunchy. Fill pita halves just before serving.

Deli roast beef slices, rolled and thinly sliced	6 oz.	170 g
Finely chopped red onion	2 tbsp.	30 mL
Finely diced dill pickle	¼ cup	60 mL
Finely shredded cabbage	3 cups	750 mL
Grated carrot	½ cup	125 mL
DRESSING		
Non-fat plain yogurt	¼ cup	60 mL
Non-fat salad dressing	¼ cup	60 mL
Creamed horseradish	1 tsp.	5 mL
Granulated sugar	¼ tsp.	1 mL
Salt	⅛ tsp.	0.5 mL
Chopped fresh parsley (optional)	1 tbsp.	15 mL
Pita breads (8 inch, 20 cm, size), cut in half	2	2

Toss first 5 ingredients in medium bowl.

Dressing: Combine first 6 ingredients in small bowl. Toss with cabbage mixture. Makes 4 cups (1 L) coleslaw.

Fill pita halves with 1 cup (250 mL) filling each. Makes 4 pita halves.

NUTRITION INFORMATION 1 pita half: 203 Calories; 2.8 g Total Fat (0.9 g Sat., 28.3 mg Cholesterol); 505 mg Sodium; 17 g Protein; 26 g Carbohydrate; 2 g Dietary Fiber

CHOICES 1 Starch; 1 Fruit & Vegetable; 2 Protein

Main Dishes

try these main course recipes that your family or friends will savor. With beef, pork, poultry, fish and pasta, there's a variety of easily prepared recipes you'll never tire of and that are also healthy and low in fat. Check out our meatless and pasta choices for options low in saturated fat and cholesterol.

Mexican Enchiladas

Just a slight bite. Use hot salsa for more spice.

Extra lean ground beef	¹/₂ lb.	225 g
Chopped onion	¹/₂ cup	125 mL
Can of diced green chilies, drained	4 oz.	114 mL
Envelope of taco seasoning mix (1¹/₄ oz., 35 g)	¹/₂	¹/₂
Can of pinto beans, drained and rinsed	14 oz.	398 mL
Salsa	¹/₂ cup	125 mL
Frozen kernel corn	¹/₃ cup	75 mL
Corn tortillas (6 inch, 15 cm, size)	12	12
Salsa	¹/₂ cup	125 mL
Grated light sharp Cheddar cheese	¹/₂ cup	125 mL

Scramble-fry beef and onion in large non-stick frying pan until no pink remains in beef.

Stir in next 5 ingredients. Heat until bubbling.

Heat tortillas, 6 at a time, wrapped in wet paper towels in microwave on high (100%) for 45 seconds. Place scant ¹/₃ cup (75 mL) filling on tortilla down center. Fold both sides over filling. Place folded side down in lightly greased 9 x 13 inch (22 x 33 cm) pan. Repeat with remaining tortillas. Keep tortillas under damp tea towel or paper towel to prevent cracking.

Drizzle with second amount of salsa and sprinkle with cheese. Cover. Bake in 350°F (175°C) oven for 15 to 20 minutes until hot. Makes 12 enchiladas.

NUTRITION INFORMATION 1 enchilada: 201 Calories; 5.4 g Total Fat (1.7 g Sat., 15.8 mg Cholesterol); 814 mg Sodium; 11 g Protein; 28 g Carbohydrate; 3 g Dietary Fiber

CHOICES 1¹/₂ Starch; ¹/₂ Fruit & Vegetable; 1 Protein

Pictured on back cover.

Baked Beef Burritos

Wonderful flavor. Baked with a minimum of oil. Serve with sour cream, salsa, tomatoes and lettuce.

Lime juice	¼ cup	60 mL
Chili sauce	¼ cup	60 mL
Garlic clove, minced	1	1
Liquid honey	1 tsp.	5 mL
Ground coriander	¼ tsp.	1 mL
Ground cumin	⅛ tsp.	0.5 mL
Dried crushed chilies	⅛ tsp.	0.5 mL
Flank steak, trimmed and scored on both sides	¾ lb.	340 g
Large red or yellow peppers (or 1 of each), thinly sliced	2	2
Medium red onions, sliced ¼ inch (6 mm) thick	2	2
Canola oil	2 tsp.	10 mL
Flour tortillas (9½ inch, 24 cm, burrito size), warmed	10	10

Combine first 7 ingredients in large sealable freezer bag. Add steak. Seal. Chill for at least two hours or overnight, turning several times. Drain marinade into small saucepan. Bring to a boil. Simmer, uncovered, for 2 minutes. Makes ¼ cup (60 mL) sauce.

Toss peppers, onion, canola oil and ½ of marinade in medium bowl.

Arrange steak, peppers and onion mixture in single layer on baking sheet. Bake in 400°F (205°C) oven for 7 to 10 minutes. Toss vegetables and turn steak over. Baste steak with remaining sauce. Bake 7 to 10 minutes until desired doneness. Thinly slice steak on diagonal across grain at sharp angle. Toss with peppers, onion and juices. Arrange ½ cup (125 mL) steak mixture on each tortilla. Add desired toppings. Fold envelope-style. Makes 10 burritos.

NUTRITION INFORMATION 1 burrito: 252 Calories; 4.3 g Total Fat (1.3 g Sat., 13.8 mg Cholesterol); 325 mg Sodium; 14 g Protein; 39 g Carbohydrate; 1 g Dietary Fiber

CHOICES 2 Starch; ½ Fruit & Vegetable; 1 Protein

Shoulder, flank and hip cuts of beef are leaner than cuts like ribs, loin or short loin. Leaner cuts tend to be less tender, which is why they are good choices for marinating.

Barbecued Beef-In-A-Bun

Done in the oven, lean beef is made tender with lots of sauce.

Flank steak, trimmed	1½ lbs.	680 g
Barbecue sauce	½ cup	125 mL
Tomato sauce	½ cup	125 mL
Garlic cloves, minced (optional)	2	2
Prepared mustard	1 tbsp.	15 mL
Worcestershire sauce	1 tsp.	5 mL
Chopped green pepper	½ cup	125 mL
Small onion, thinly sliced	1	1
Whole wheat buns, toasted	8-10	8-10

Lay whole flank steak in bottom of lightly sprayed small roaster or 3 quart (3 L) casserole.

Combine next 6 ingredients in small bowl. Pour over steak.

Top with onion slices. Cover. Bake in 300°F (150°C) oven for about 2 hours until meat is very tender. Remove steak. Let cool slightly. Thinly slice on diagonal. Return to roaster. Stir.

Pile about ⅓ cup (75 mL) steak and sauce onto each bun to serve. Makes 3½ cups (875 mL).

NUTRITION INFORMATION ⅓ cup (75 mL): 191 Calories; 5.9 g Total Fat (2.3 g Sat., 26.4 mg Cholesterol); 393 mg Sodium; 17 g Protein; 17 g Carbohydrate; 3 g Dietary Fiber

CHOICES 1 Starch; 2 Protein

To Make Ahead: Fill buns and wrap in plastic wrap and foil. Label. Freeze. To serve, defrost at room temperature for 3½ to 4 hours. Good cold, or wrap in paper towel and microwave on medium (50%) for 30 seconds to 1 minute until hot.

Green Pepper Beef Loaf

Delicious cold the next day, in a sandwich or broken up and heated to fill a flour tortilla. Just add plenty of salsa, tomatoes and lettuce.

Medium green pepper, cut into chunks	1	1
Skim evaporated milk	½ cup	125 mL
Large egg	1	1
Chopped onion	¼ cup	60 mL
Onion salt	1 tsp.	5 mL
Freshly ground pepper, sprinkle		
Parsley flakes	1 tsp.	5 mL
Extra lean ground beef	1½ lbs.	680 g
Fine dry bread crumbs	½ cup	125 mL

(continued on next page)

• MAIN DISHES •

Process first 7 ingredients in blender until pepper and onion are quite finely chopped. Pour into medium bowl.

Add ground beef and bread crumbs. Mix very well. Pack into foil-lined, greased 9 x 5 x 3 inch (22 x 12.5 x 7.5 cm) loaf pan. Bake, uncovered, in 350°F (175°C) oven for 1½ to 2 hours until no pink remains in beef. Drain off liquid. Turn out onto plate. Peel off foil. Cuts into 10 slices.

NUTRITION INFORMATION 1 slice: 212 Calories; 10.2 g Total Fat (3.9 g Sat., 76.9 mg Cholesterol); 256 mg Sodium; 22 g Protein; 7 g Carbohydrate; trace Dietary Fiber

CHOICES ½ Starch; 3 Protein

Beef And Sprout Stir-Fry

Crunchy with lots of sauce to serve on noodles or rice.

SAUCE		
Water	½ cup	125 mL
Cornstarch	1 tbsp.	15 mL
Low-sodium soy sauce	¼ cup	60 mL
Garlic powder (optional)	⅛ tsp.	0.5 mL
Canola oil	2 tsp.	10 mL
Lean sirloin (or flank) steak, trimmed and cut crosswise into very thin slices	¾ lb.	340 g
Garlic cloves, minced	2	2
Sliced fresh mushrooms	1 cup	250 mL
Thinly sliced celery	½ cup	125 mL
Coarsely shredded carrot	½ cup	125 mL
Chopped green onion	½ cup	125 mL
Fresh bean sprouts	3 cups	750 mL

Sauce: Stir first 4 ingredients in small bowl. Set aside.

Heat canola oil in non-stick frying pan or wok on medium-high. Add steak and garlic. Stir-fry for 3 minutes. Add mushrooms, celery and carrot. Stir-fry for 4 minutes.

Stir sauce. Add to steak mixture. Add green onion and sprouts. Heat and stir for 2 minutes until boiling and thickened. Makes 4 cups (1 L).

NUTRITION INFORMATION 1 cup (250 mL): 213 Calories; 8.9 g Total Fat (2.9 g Sat., 34.6 mg Cholesterol); 736 mg Sodium; 23 g Protein; 11 g Carbohydrate; 2 g Dietary Fiber

CHOICES 1 Fruit & Vegetable; 3 Protein; ½ Fat & Oil

Fast-Fix Beef

Using readily available broccoli slaw makes this very quick.

SAUCE

Water	**1 cup**	**250 mL**
Low-sodium soy sauce	**¼ cup**	**60 mL**
Hoisin sauce	**1 tbsp.**	**15 mL**
Cornstarch	**2 tbsp.**	**30 mL**
Canola oil	**2 tsp.**	**10 mL**
Sirloin (or flank) steak, trimmed and cut crosswise into very thin slices	**¾ lb.**	**340 g**
Garlic cloves, minced	**2**	**2**
Packaged broccoli (or regular cabbage) slaw	**3 cups**	**750 mL**
Green onions, sliced	**3**	**3**
Fresh (or 10 oz., 285 g, frozen, thawed and drained) pea pods	**1¼ cups**	**300 mL**
Instant Chinese-style noodles (2 squares), broken up	**4 oz.**	**113 g**

Sauce: Combine all 4 ingredients in small bowl. Set aside.

Heat canola oil in large frying pan or wok on medium-high. Add beef and garlic. Stir-fry for 1 minute. Add slaw, onion and pea pods. Stir-fry for 3 minutes.

Stir sauce. Add to beef mixture. Stir in noodles. Heat and stir for 3 minutes until boiling and thickened. Makes 6 cups (1.5 L).

NUTRITION INFORMATION 1 cup (250 mL): 227 Calories; 6.8 g Total Fat (2.1 g Sat., 41 mg Cholesterol); 805 mg Sodium; 19 g Protein; 23 g Carbohydrate; 3 g Dietary Fiber

CHOICES 1 Starch; 1 Fruit & Vegetable; 2 Protein

Grilled Hoisin Flank Steak

Marinade is reduced and doubles as a flavorful baste.

Low-sodium soy sauce	**3 tbsp.**	**50 mL**
Hoisin sauce	**3 tbsp.**	**50 mL**
Water	**½ cup**	**125 mL**
Green onion	**1**	**1**
Hot chili paste	**½ tsp.**	**2 mL**
Garlic cloves	**3**	**3**
Gingerroot, peeled	**½ slice**	**½ slice**
Dry red (or alcohol-free) wine	**¼ cup**	**60 mL**
Lemon juice	**2 tbsp.**	**30 mL**
Flank steak, trimmed and scored on both sides	**1½ lbs.**	**680 g**

(continued on next page)

Purée first 9 ingredients in blender. Pour into large sealable freezer bag. Add steak. Seal. Chill for several hours or overnight, turning several times. Drain marinade into small saucepan. Bring to a boil. Heat until reduced by half and slightly thickened. Makes ½ cup (125 mL) sauce. Grill steak over medium-high heat on barbecue for about 5 minutes per side, basting several times with sauce, until desired doneness. Thinly slice across grain at slight angle. Discard any remaining sauce. Serves 6.

NUTRITION INFORMATION 1 serving: 219 Calories; 8.4 g Total Fat (3.6 g Sat., 46.1 mg Cholesterol); 747 mg Sodium; 26 g Protein; 7 g Carbohydrate; trace Dietary Fiber

CHOICES ½ Sugar; 3½ Protein

Pictured on page 72.

Variation: Grill steak on medium-high in indoor double-sided grill. Heat for about 10 minutes, basting several times, until desired doneness.

Vegetable Gravy

This versatile sauce can be used as a stroganoff sauce for beef or chicken just by adding a little non-fat or light sour cream. Also good as a sauce for meatballs. Make a double batch of base and freeze to always have on hand.

Water	3 cups	750 mL
Vegetable bouillon powder	1 tbsp.	15 mL
Garlic cloves, peeled	8	8
Large carrot, cut into 1 inch (2.5 cm) pieces	1	1
Large celery rib, cut into 1 inch (2.5 cm) pieces	1	1
Large onion, chopped	1	1
Cornstarch (see Note)	2 tbsp.	30 mL
Water	¼ cup	60 mL
Light sour cream (optional)	¼ cup	60 mL

Bring water to a boil in large saucepan. Add bouillon powder, garlic cloves, carrot, celery and onion. Cover. Simmer for about 40 minutes until vegetables are very soft. Purée in saucepan with hand blender. Freeze at this point if desired.

Combine cornstarch and water in small dish. Stir into purée. Heat and stir on medium, until boiling and slightly thickened. Stir in sour cream. Makes 4 cups (1 L).

NUTRITION INFORMATION ½ cup (125 mL): 29 Calories; 0.2 g Total Fat (0.1 g Sat., 0.1 mg Cholesterol); 234 mg Sodium; 1 g Protein; 6 g Carbohydrate; 1 g Dietary Fiber

CHOICES ½ Fruit & Vegetable

Note: To freeze, omit cornstarch and water. Freeze in 2 cup (500 mL) portions. After thawing, thicken with 1 tbsp. (15 mL) cornstarch and 2 tbsp. (30 mL) water.

Chicken Stew

For best results, use a deep non-stick electric frying pan for this recipe.

Chicken parts, skin removed	3 lbs.	1.4 kg
Garlic powder, sprinkle		
Freshly ground pepper, sprinkle		
Water	²/₃ cup	150 mL
Lemon juice	2 tbsp.	30 mL
Prepared orange juice	2 tbsp.	30 mL
Chicken bouillon powder	2 tsp.	10 mL
Dried rosemary, crushed	1 tsp.	5 mL
Parsley flakes	2 tsp.	10 mL
Bay leaf	1	1
Medium red potatoes, quartered (about 1¹/₂ lbs., 680 g)	4	4
Baby carrots	3 cups	750 mL
Can of skim evaporated milk	13¹/₂ oz.	385 mL
Cornstarch	3 tbsp.	50 mL

Cook chicken in non-stick electric frying pan at 425°F (220°C) on all sides until browned, sprinkling with garlic powder and pepper while cooking.

Add next 9 ingredients. Stir to coat. Cover. Cook at 350°F (175°C) for 30 to 35 minutes, stirring twice, until no pink remains in chicken and juices run clear. Remove and discard bay leaf.

Combine evaporated milk and cornstarch in small bowl. Add to chicken mixture. Heat and stir until boiling and thickened. Makes 8 cups (2 L).

NUTRITION INFORMATION 1¹/₄ cups (300 mL): 312 Calories; 3.6 g Total Fat (0.9 g Sat., 75.1 mg Cholesterol); 407 mg Sodium; 31 g Protein; 39 g Carbohydrate; 4 g Dietary Fiber

CHOICES 1¹/₂ Starch; 1 Fruit & Vegetable; 1 Milk; 3 Protein

Special Plum Chicken

Lots of good plum flavor and a spicy bite in the sauce. Spoon sauce on chicken or rice.

Chicken parts, skin removed	3 lbs.	1.4 kg
Jars of strained plums (baby food), 4¹/₂ oz. (128 mL) each	3	3
Garlic cloves, minced	2	2
Ground ginger	1 tsp.	5 mL
Chili sauce	2 tbsp.	30 mL
Lemon juice	1 tsp.	5 mL
Brown sugar, packed	1 tsp.	5 mL
Chili paste (optional)	¹/₂ tsp.	2 mL

(continued on next page)

Arrange chicken in single layer in 9 x 13 inch (22 x 33 cm) foil-lined baking dish that has been lightly sprayed with cooking spray.

Combine remaining 7 ingredients in small bowl. Pour over chicken, making sure to get some on each piece. Bake, uncovered, in 350°F (175°C) oven for about 50 minutes, basting 3 to 4 times with sauce during last half of baking time. Serves 4.

NUTRITION INFORMATION 1 serving: 247 Calories; 3.9 g Total Fat (1 g Sat., 91.2 mg Cholesterol); 228 mg Sodium; 29 g Protein; 24 g Carbohydrate; 2 g Dietary Fiber

CHOICES 2 Fruit & Vegetable; 4 Protein

Chicken Supreme

Lots of sauce to flavor rice or noodles.

SAUCE		
Cold water	1 cup	250 mL
Cornstarch	2 tbsp.	30 mL
Low-sodium soy sauce	3 tbsp.	50 mL
Hoisin sauce	2 tbsp.	30 mL
Dried crushed chilies	1/2 tsp.	2 mL
Onion powder	1/2 tsp.	2 mL
Canola oil	2 tsp.	10 mL
Boneless, skinless chicken breast halves (about 3), cut into bite-size pieces	3/4 lb.	340 g
Canola oil	1 tsp.	5 mL
Thinly sliced vegetables (such as carrots, celery, broccoli, cauliflower and green peppers)	6 cups	1.5 L
Medium onion, peeled and cut lengthwise into wedges	1	1
Garlic cloves, minced	2	2

Sauce: Combine first 6 ingredients in small bowl. Set aside.

Heat first amount of canola oil in non-stick frying pan or wok on medium-high. Add chicken. Stir-fry for about 4 minutes until no pink remains in chicken. Remove to bowl.

Heat second amount of canola oil in same frying pan or wok. Stir-fry vegetables, onion and garlic for about 8 minutes until tender-crisp. Add chicken. Stir sauce. Add to chicken mixture. Heat and stir until boiling and thickened. Makes 6 cups (1.5 L).

NUTRITION INFORMATION 1 cup (250 mL): 147 Calories; 3.4 g Total Fat (0.4 g Sat., 32.9 mg Cholesterol); 889 mg Sodium; 16 g Protein; 14 g Carbohydrate; 3 g Dietary Fiber

CHOICES 1 1/2 Fruit & Vegetable; 2 Protein

Curried Chicken And Bulgur

A delicious one-dish meal. Even leftovers taste good.

Canola oil	2 tsp.	10 mL
Boneless, skinless chicken breast halves (about 3), cut into bite-size pieces	¾ lb.	340 g
Medium onion, chopped	1	1
Large celery rib, diced	1	1
Medium carrots, coarsely grated	2	2
Curry powder	½ tsp.	2 mL
Ground cumin	¼ tsp.	1 mL
Ground cardamom	¼ tsp.	1 mL
Can of condensed chicken broth	10 oz.	284 mL
Water	¾ cup	175 mL
Bulgur wheat (6 oz., 170 g)	1 cup	250 mL
Light raisins	2 tbsp.	30 mL
Ground cinnamon	⅛ tsp.	0.5 mL
Salt	⅛ tsp.	0.5 mL
Finely chopped toasted pecans (or walnuts)	2 tbsp.	30 mL

Heat canola oil in non-stick frying pan on medium-high. Sauté chicken and onion until no pink remains in chicken and onion is soft.

Stir in celery, carrot, curry, cumin and cardamom. Heat for about 3 minutes until fragrant and carrot is softened.

Add next 6 ingredients. Cover. Simmer for 15 to 20 minutes until bulgur is tender. Fluff with fork.

Sprinkle with pecans. Makes 5 cups (1.25 L). Serves 4.

NUTRITION INFORMATION 1¼ cups (300 mL): 334 Calories; 7.4 g Total Fat (1 g Sat., 50.1 mg Cholesterol); 646 mg Sodium; 29 g Protein; 40 g Carbohydrate; 9 g Dietary Fiber

CHOICES 2 Starch; 1 Fruit & Vegetable; 3 Protein

Pictured on page 89.

Chicken Chili

Serve on brown rice or as is with salad. Uses Tomato Vegetable Sauce, page 106.

Lean ground chicken	¾ lb.	340 g
Finely chopped celery	½ cup	125 mL
Container of Tomato Vegetable Sauce (3 cups, 750 mL), page 106, thawed	1	1
Chili powder	2 tsp.	10 mL
Can of red kidney beans, drained	14 oz.	398 mL

(continued on next page)

Scramble-fry chicken and celery in non-stick frying pan until starting to brown. Drain. Add Tomato Vegetable Sauce, chili powder and kidney beans. Cover. Simmer for 30 minutes to blend flavors. Makes 5 cups (1.25 L).

NUTRITION INFORMATION 1¼ cups (300 mL): 239 Calories; 3.1 g Total Fat (0.5 g Sat., 49.3 mg Cholesterol); 472 mg Sodium; 27 g Protein; 27 g Carbohydrate; 8 g Dietary Fiber

CHOICES 1 Starch; 1 Fruit & Vegetable; 3 Protein

Oriental Chicken Packets

This recipe can easily be doubled or tripled. No dirty pans to wash up after!

Thinly sliced onion	½ cup	125 mL
Julienned carrot	¾ cup	175 mL
Slivered green pepper	½ cup	125 mL
Fresh bean sprouts (6 oz., 170 g)	2 cups	500 mL
Couscous	6 tbsp.	100 mL
Boneless, skinless chicken breast halves (about 4 oz., 113 g, each)	2	2
Brown sugar, packed	1 tsp.	5 mL
Ground ginger	¼ tsp.	1 mL
Garlic powder	¼ tsp.	1 mL
Hoisin sauce	1 tbsp.	15 mL
Water	¾ cup	175 mL
Ketchup	1 tbsp.	15 mL
Freshly ground pepper, sprinkle		

Toss first 4 ingredients in medium bowl. Divide between two 12 × 24 inch (30 × 60 cm) heavy-duty foil sheets.

Sprinkle 3 tbsp. (50 mL) couscous on each sheet. Place whole chicken breast on top.

Combine next 6 ingredients in small bowl. Drizzle ½ (about 7 tbsp., 115 mL, each) on chicken breast. Sprinkle with pepper. Bring both 12 inch (30 cm) ends up and together over chicken. Fold together several times to seal. Fold sides in at an angle. Roll up to seal and create handles for removing from oven. Repeat for second packet. Cook directly on center rack in 400°F (205°C) oven for 40 minutes. Makes 2 packets.

NUTRITION INFORMATION 1 packet: 371 Calories; 2.1 g Total Fat (0.5 g Sat., 65.5 mg Cholesterol); 565 mg Sodium; 35 g Protein; 53 g Carbohydrate; 5 g Dietary Fiber

CHOICES 2 Starch; 2 Fruit & Vegetable; 4 Protein

Chicken And Black Bean Stir-Fry

Make the sauce a day before so you're all ready to go for the stir-fry. Serve with brown or white rice. See Tip, page 87.

BLACK BEAN SAUCE

Dried black beans (see Note)	⅓ cup	75 mL
Boiling water	3 cups	750 mL
Garlic cloves, minced	2	2
Low-sodium soy sauce	1 tbsp.	15 mL
Freshly grated gingerroot	1 tsp.	5 mL
Water	¾ cup	175 mL
Sherry (or alcohol-free sherry)	2 tbsp.	30 mL
Canola oil	1 tsp.	5 mL
Boneless, skinless chicken breast halves (about 3), cut into long, thin strips	¾ lb.	340 g
Canola oil	1 tsp.	5 mL
Carrots, thinly cut on diagonal	½ cup	125 mL
Broccoli stems, thinly cut on diagonal	⅔ cup	150 mL
Small onion, sliced lengthwise	1	1
Sliced fresh mushrooms	⅔ cup	150 mL
Water	1 tbsp.	15 mL
Broccoli florets, cut into bite-size pieces	1½ cups	375 mL
Fresh pea pods (about 4 oz., 113 g)	20	20

Black Bean Sauce: Cook dried beans in boiling water in small uncovered saucepan for 70 minutes. Drain. Rinse. Remove 3 tbsp. (50 mL). Freeze remainder in 3 tbsp. (50 mL) portions for future sauce.

Bring beans, garlic, soy sauce, ginger, water and sherry to a boil in small uncovered saucepan. Boil for about 15 minutes until reduced by half. Mash beans slightly with back of spoon while cooking. Makes ⅓ cup (75 mL).

Heat first amount of canola oil in non-stick frying pan or wok. Stir-fry chicken on high for 2 to 3 minutes until no pink remains in chicken. Remove to plate.

Heat second amount of canola oil in same frying pan or wok. Stir-fry carrot and broccoli stems for 2 minutes. Add onion and mushrooms. Stir-fry for 2 minutes. Add water, broccoli florets and pea pods. Stir. Cover. Cook for 2 to 3 minutes until broccoli is tender-crisp. Add bean sauce and chicken. Stir to coat. Makes 4½ cups (1.1 L).

NUTRITION INFORMATION 1 cup (250 mL): 173 Calories; 3.4 g Total Fat (0.5 g Sat., 43.8 mg Cholesterol); 134 mg Sodium; 22 g Protein; 14 g Carbohydrate; 3 g Dietary Fiber

CHOICES 1½ Fruit & Vegetable; 3 Protein

Pictured on page 89.

Note: To save time, soak beans overnight. Drain. Bring beans and water to a boil in small uncovered saucepan. Cook on medium for 15 to 20 minutes. To save even more time, use 3 tbsp. (50 mL) drained canned beans. Freeze remainder in small batches for future use.

Curried Chicken And Fruit

Fast and delicious. Serve on couscous or rice.

Boneless, skinless chicken breast halves (about 3), cut into bite-size pieces	¾ lb.	340 g
Chopped onion	½ cup	125 mL
Garlic cloves, minced	2	2
Canola oil	2 tsp.	10 mL
Can of stewed tomatoes, with juice, chopped	14 oz.	398 mL
Water	½ cup	125 mL
Diced dried apricots	¼ cup	60 mL
Raisins	¼ cup	60 mL
Lemon juice	2 tsp.	10 mL
Curry paste (available in Asian section of grocery store)	2 tsp.	10 mL
Chicken bouillon powder	1 tsp.	5 mL
Ground cinnamon	¼ tsp.	1 mL
Bay leaf	1	1
Skim evaporated milk	½ cup	125 mL
Cornstarch	2 tsp.	10 mL

Sauté chicken, onion and garlic in canola oil in large frying pan for 5 minutes until onion is soft.

Stir in next 9 ingredients. Bring to a boil. Reduce heat. Cover. Simmer for 30 minutes. Remove and discard bay leaf.

Combine evaporated milk and cornstarch in small dish. Add to chicken mixture while stirring. Bring to a boil. Heat for 1 minute until slightly thickened. Makes 4 cups (1 L).

NUTRITION INFORMATION 1 cup (250 mL): 244 Calories; 4.4 g Total Fat (0.6 g Sat., 50.6 mg Cholesterol); 533 mg Sodium; 24 g Protein; 28 g Carbohydrate; 3 g Dietary Fiber

CHOICES 2 Fruit & Vegetable; ½ Milk; 3 Protein

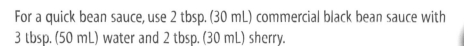

For a quick bean sauce, use 2 tbsp. (30 mL) commercial black bean sauce with 3 tbsp. (50 mL) water and 2 tbsp. (30 mL) sherry.

Caesar Chicken

Intense Caesar flavor. Only requires plain rice or noodles and a salad to complete the meal.

Non-fat mayonnaise (or salad dressing)	¼ **cup**	**60 mL**
Light Caesar salad dressing	¼ **cup**	**60 mL**
Garlic cloves, minced	**2**	**2**
Dry mustard	½ **tsp.**	**2 mL**
Parsley flakes	½ **tsp.**	**2 mL**
Freshly ground pepper, sprinkle		
Boneless, skinless chicken breast halves (about 4 oz., 113 g, each)	**4**	**4**
Fine dry bread crumbs	⅓ **cup**	**75 mL**
Grated light Parmesan cheese	**2 tbsp.**	**30 mL**
No-stick cooking spray		

Combine first 6 ingredients in small bowl. Makes ½ cup (125 mL) marinade. Transfer to large sealable freezer bag.

Flatten breasts slightly. Place in bag. Turn to coat. Seal. Chill for several hours or overnight.

Combine crumbs and cheese on dinner plate. Remove chicken breasts from bag one at a time, leaving as much dressing on as possible. Coat well in crumb mixture. Place on greased baking sheet. Spray surface with cooking spray. Bake, uncovered, in center of 375°F (190°C) oven for 25 minutes until no pink remains in chicken and juices run clear. Serves 4.

NUTRITION INFORMATION 1 serving: 224 Calories; 4.9 g Total Fat (1 g Sat., 69.3 mg Cholesterol); 490 mg Sodium; 29 g Protein; 14 g Carbohydrate; trace Dietary Fiber

CHOICES 1 Starch; 4 Protein

1. Chicken And Black Bean Stir-Fry, page 86
2. Curried Chicken And Bulgur, page 84
3. Turkey Vegetable Meatloaf, page 115
4. Turkey Breast With Rice Stuffing, page 114

Chicken 'N' Rice

Wholesome flavor in this time-honored comfort dish. Only 10 minutes to put together, and then forget about it for over an hour!

Boiling water	2¹/₂ cups	625 mL
Dehydrated mixed vegetables	²/₃ cup	150 mL
Chicken bouillon powder	1 tbsp.	15 mL
Garlic clove, minced (optional)	1	1
Poultry seasoning	¹/₂ tsp.	2 mL
Ground rosemary	¹/₁₆ tsp.	0.5 mL
Celery salt	¹/₂ tsp.	2 mL
Long grain brown rice	1¹/₂ cups	375 mL
Chicken parts, skin removed	1¹/₂ lbs.	680 g
Paprika	¹/₂ tsp.	2 mL
Freshly ground pepper, sprinkle		

Combine first 8 ingredients in lightly sprayed 2 quart (2 L) casserole.

Arrange chicken over rice mixture. Do not stir. Sprinkle with paprika and pepper. Cover tightly. Bake in 350°F (175°C) oven for 75 minutes. Stir. Cover. Bake for 15 to 20 minutes until rice is tender. Serves 6.

NUTRITION INFORMATION 1 serving: 318 Calories; 3.5 g Total Fat (0.8 g Sat., 37.8 mg Cholesterol); 525 mg Sodium; 19 g Protein; 53 g Carbohydrate; 6 g Dietary Fiber

CHOICES 2¹/₂ Starch; 1¹/₂ Fruit & Vegetable; 2 Protein

1. Tuna Casserole, page 96
2. Fresh Fruit Salsa, page 95
3. Jambalaya, page 97
4. Orange Codfish, page 98

Fish Cakes

Serve with Tzatziki, page 94, or Roasted Red Pepper Sauce, page 93.

Cod (or snapper) fillets	$^3/_4$ lb.	340 g
Skim milk	$^1/_3$ cup	75 mL
Bay leaf	1	1
Medium potatoes, peeled and cut into small chunks (about $^3/_4$ lb., 340 g)	2	2
Water	$^1/_2$ cup	125 mL
Salt	$^1/_2$ tsp.	2 mL
Non-fat plain yogurt	3 tbsp.	50 mL
Egg whites (large), fork-beaten	2	2
Dijon mustard	1 tbsp.	15 mL
Worcestershire sauce	1 tsp.	5 mL
Green onions, finely sliced	2	2
Salt	$^1/_4$ tsp.	1 mL
Pepper	$^1/_8$ tsp.	0.5 mL
Dill weed	$^1/_2$ tsp.	2 mL
Parsley flakes	$^1/_2$ tsp.	2 mL
Fine dry bread crumbs	$^2/_3$ cup	150 mL

Put fish, milk and bay leaf in large non-stick frying pan. Cover. Poach on medium for 3 to 4 minutes until fish is opaque and flakes easily. Drain well. Remove and discard bay leaf. Chill fish.

Place potato, water and salt in small saucepan. Cover. Bring to a boil. Heat for 15 minutes until soft. Drain, reserving about $^1/_4$ cup (60 mL) water. Mash until no lumps remain.

Combine next 9 ingredients in small bowl. Add to potato. Mix well. Add fish. Stir, flaking fish with fork. Form into 10 patties.

Place bread crumbs on sheet of waxed paper. Coat each patty. Place on greased baking sheet. Spray patties well with cooking spray. Bake, uncovered, in 375°F (190°C) oven for 20 minutes until firm, golden brown and crisp. Makes 10 patties.

NUTRITION INFORMATION 1 patty: 92 Calories; 0.7 g Total Fat (0.2 g Sat., 14.9 mg Cholesterol); 190 mg Sodium; 9 g Protein; 12 g Carbohydrate; 1 g Dietary Fiber

CHOICES 1 Starch; 1 Protein

EASY FISH CAKES: Omit cod, milk and bay leaf. Use two $7^1/_2$ oz. (213 g) cans of salmon, drained. Omit potatoes and first amount of salt. Use $1^1/_2$ cups (375 mL) leftover mashed potatoes.

Roasted Red Pepper Sauce

Try this on Fish Cakes, page 92, poached fish fillets or in a sandwich wrap. Will keep covered in refrigerator for up to one week.

Frozen egg product, thawed (see Note)	$^1/_2$ cup	125 mL
Garlic cloves	2	2
Non-fat mayonnaise (not salad dressing)	$^1/_2$ cup	125 mL
Lemon juice	2 tsp.	10 mL
Salt	$^1/_8$ tsp.	0.5 mL
Cayenne pepper, sprinkle		
Olive oil, heated to 250°-300°F (120°-150°C)	$^1/_3$ cup	75 mL
Can of roasted red peppers, drained and blotted dry, cut into strips (see Tip, below)	14 oz.	398 mL

Process egg substitute and garlic in blender until garlic is finely chopped. Add mayonnaise, lemon juice, salt and cayenne. Process, scraping down sides if necessary, until smooth.

With blender running, slowly and carefully add hot olive oil in steady stream through hole in lid.

With blender running, add red pepper strips, 1 at a time, allowing each piece to completely blend before adding another, periodically scraping down sides. Makes 2 cups (500 mL).

NUTRITION INFORMATION 2 tbsp. (30 mL): 52 Calories; 4.6 g Total Fat (0.6 g Sat., 0 mg Cholesterol); 82 mg Sodium; 1 g Protein; 2 g Carbohydrate; trace Dietary Fiber

CHOICES 1 Fat & Oil

Note: 4 tbsp. (50 mL) =1 large egg

To roast peppers in oven, place on baking sheet under the broiler, turning frequently, until skin is blistered and blackened. Cover with plastic wrap. Let sweat for about 15 minutes until cool enough to handle. Remove and discard skin from peppers by scraping them.

Salmon Rice Mélange

Make rice the night before, and this casserole goes together in minutes.

Package of long grain and wild rice mix	**6^1/$_2$ oz.**	**180 g**
Canola oil	**2 tsp.**	**10 mL**
Chopped onion	**^{1}/$_2$ cup**	**125 mL**
Chopped celery	**^{1}/$_2$ cup**	**125 mL**
All-purpose flour	**2 tbsp.**	**30 mL**
No-salt herb seasoning (such as Mrs. Dash)	**^{1}/$_2$ tsp.**	**2 mL**
Skim evaporated milk	**^{3}/$_4$ cup**	**175 mL**
Skim milk	**^{3}/$_4$ cup**	**175 mL**
Low-sodium soy sauce	**1 tbsp.**	**15 mL**
Frozen peas	**1 cup**	**250 mL**
Can of red salmon, drained, round bones removed	**7^1/$_2$ oz.**	**213 g**
Fine dry bread crumbs	**^{1}/$_4$ cup**	**60 mL**
Grated light Monterey Jack cheese	**^{1}/$_2$ cup**	**125 mL**

Cook rice mix as per package directions without margarine.

Heat canola oil in non-stick frying pan. Cook onion and celery for 5 minutes until soft. Sprinkle flour and herb seasoning over top. Stir for 1 minute. Slowly add both milks, stirring constantly, until smooth. Stir in soy sauce and peas until boiling and thickened. Add rice and salmon. Stir gently. Turn into greased 1^1/$_2$ quart (1.5 L) casserole.

Combine bread crumbs and cheese. Sprinkle over top. Bake, uncovered, in 350°F (175°C) oven for 20 to 30 minutes until edges are bubbling and casserole is hot in center. Serves 6.

NUTRITION INFORMATION 1 serving: 457 Calories; 7.2 g Total Fat (4.1 g Sat., 35.8 mg Cholesterol); 633 mg Sodium; 19 g Protein; 40 g Carbohydrate; 2 g Dietary Fiber

CHOICES 2 Starch; ^{1}/$_2$ Fruit & Vegetable; 1 Milk; 1^1/$_2$ Protein; ^{1}/$_2$ Fat & Oil

Tzatziki

Always a favorite and so healthy when using non-fat Yogurt Cheese, page 75. Serve on warmed and torn pita bread or with Fish Cakes, page 92.

Grated English cucumber, with peel	**1 cup**	**250 mL**
Salt	**1^1/$_2$ tsp.**	**7 mL**
Yogurt Cheese, page 75	**1 cup**	**250 mL**
Granulated sugar	**^{1}/$_4$ tsp.**	**1 mL**
Garlic clove(s), minced	**1-2**	**1-2**
Salt	**^{1}/$_4$ tsp.**	**1 mL**
Freshly ground pepper, sprinkle		

(continued on next page)

Place cucumber in colander over small bowl. Sprinkle with salt. Drain in refrigerator for 2 hours. Squeeze out excess moisture. Discard liquid. Empty cucumber into medium bowl.

Stir in remaining 5 ingredients. Cover. Chill for 1 to 2 hours to blend flavors. Makes 1¹/₂ cups (375 mL).

NUTRITION INFORMATION 1 tbsp. (15 mL): 12 Calories; 0.3 g Total Fat (0.2 g Sat., 1.1 mg Cholesterol); 121 mg Sodium; 1 g Protein; 1 g Carbohydrate; trace Dietary Fiber

CHOICES Extra

Fresh Fruit Salsa

A very good condiment for roast pork or grilled fish. Will keep in the refrigerator for up to 4 days.

Ripe medium mango	1	1
Ripe large papaya	1	1
Finely chopped red onion	¹/₃ cup	75 mL
Small red pepper, diced	1	1
Lime juice (fresh is best)	¹/₃ cup	75 mL
Diced English cucumber, with peel	³/₄ cup	175 mL
Chopped fresh cilantro (or mint leaves)	1 tbsp.	15 mL
Unsweetened applesauce	²/₃ cup	150 mL
Granulated sugar	1 tsp.	5 mL
Ground cinnamon	¹/₄ tsp.	1 mL

Fresh mint, for garnish

Peel and dice mango and papaya, with juices, into medium bowl.

Stir in next 8 ingredients. Cover. Chill for 1 hour to blend flavors.

Garnish with mint leaves if desired. Makes 3¹/₂ cups (875 mL).

NUTRITION INFORMATION ¹/₄ cup (60 mL): 30 Calories; 0.1 g Total Fat (trace Sat., 0 mg Cholesterol); 2 mg Sodium; trace Protein; 8 g Carbohydrate; 1 g Dietary Fiber

CHOICES 1 Fruit & Vegetable

Pictured on front cover and on page 90.

If mango and papaya are unavailable, try the canned varieties. Or substitute ripe peaches, nectarines, honeydew melon or cantaloupe.

Tuna Casserole

An old standby lightened up in calories and fat grams.

Finely chopped onion	2 tbsp.	30 mL
Chopped fresh mushrooms	1/2 cup	125 mL
Diced red pepper	1/2 cup	125 mL
Canola oil	2 tsp.	10 mL
All-purpose flour	2 tbsp.	30 mL
Skim evaporated milk	1 cup	250 mL
Skim milk	1 cup	250 mL
Seasoned salt	1/2 tsp.	2 mL
No-salt herb seasoning (such as Mrs. Dash)	1 tsp.	5 mL
Freshly ground pepper, generous sprinkle		
Frozen peas, thawed and drained	1 cup	250 mL
Can of white tuna, packed in water, drained and broken into chunks	6 oz.	170 g
Medium no-yolk noodles	3 cups	750 mL
Water	3 qts.	3 L
Whole wheat bread slice, processed into crumbs	1	1
Grated light sharp Cheddar cheese	1/2 cup	125 mL

Fresh dill, for garnish

Sauté onion, mushrooms and red pepper in canola oil in large non-stick frying pan until onion is softened. Sprinkle with flour. Stir well. Cook for about 1 minute. Slowly add both milks, stirring constantly, until boiled and just thickened. Stir in seasoned salt, herb seasoning and pepper. Remove from heat. Stir in peas and tuna.

Cook noodles in boiling water in large uncovered pot or Dutch oven for 8 minutes until tender but firm. Drain well. Pour into greased 2 quart (2 L) casserole. Gently fold in tuna mixture.

Combine bread crumbs and cheese. Sprinkle over casserole. Cover. Bake in 350°F (175°C) oven for 30 minutes until bubbling.

Garnish with dill if desired. Serves 6.

NUTRITION INFORMATION 1 serving: 248 Calories; 4.9 g Total Fat (1.7 g Sat., 18.5 mg Cholesterol); 400 mg Sodium; 19 g Protein; 32 g Carbohydrate; 2 g Dietary Fiber

CHOICES 1 1/2 Starch; 1/2 Fruit & Vegetable; 1 Milk; 1 1/2 Protein

Pictured on page 90.

 Grated light sharp Cheddar cheese provides a big hit of flavor without all the fat of regular Cheddar cheese. Try other light cheeses on the market to find great taste that's not heavy on fat grams.

Jambalaya

Add more cayenne spice or hot pepper liquid for some real Cajun heat!

Olive oil	1 tbsp.	15 mL
Chopped onion	1 cup	250 mL
Chopped celery	1 cup	250 mL
Garlic clove, minced	1	1
Chopped mixed bell peppers	1 cup	250 mL
Boneless, skinless chicken breast halves (about 3), cut into bite-size chunks	$^3/_4$ lb.	340 g
Uncooked long grain brown rice	$1^1/_4$ cups	300 mL
Water	2 cups	500 mL
Chicken bouillon powder	1 tbsp.	15 mL
Can of stewed tomatoes, with juice, cut up	14 oz.	398 mL
Hot pepper sauce	$^1/_4$-$^1/_2$ tsp.	1-2 mL
Pepper	$^1/_4$ tsp.	1 mL
Dried thyme	$^1/_4$ tsp.	1 mL
Dried whole oregano	$^1/_4$ tsp.	1 mL
Cayenne pepper	$^1/_{16}$-$^1/_8$ tsp.	0.5 mL
Medium raw shrimp, peeled and deveined (4 oz., 113 g)	12	12
Diced turkey kielbasa (or other spiced cooked lean sausage), about 3 oz. (85 g)	$^1/_2$ cup	125 mL
Sliced green onion	$^1/_4$ cup	60 mL

Heat olive oil in large non-stick frying pan. Add onion, celery, garlic and peppers. Sauté for 5 minutes on medium.

Add chicken and rice. Sauté for 5 minutes until no pink remains in chicken. Turn into lightly sprayed 3 quart (3 L) casserole.

Combine next 8 ingredients in medium saucepan. Bring to a boil. Pour over chicken mixture. Stir gently. Cover. Bake in 350°F (175°C) oven for 45 minutes.

Stir in shrimp, sausage and green onion. Cover. Bake for 10 minutes until rice is tender. Makes 8 cups (2 L). Serves 6.

NUTRITION INFORMATION 1 serving: 321 Calories; 7.4 g Total Fat (1.7 g Sat., 71.5 mg Cholesterol); 791 mg Sodium; 22 g Protein; 42 g Carbohydrate; 3 g Dietary Fiber

CHOICES 2 Starch; 1 Fruit & Vegetable; 2 Protein; $^1/_2$ Fat & Oil

Jambalaya is a favorite dish of New Orleans. This family-pleasing treat is a great way to use up leftover rice, chicken or ham. If the shrimp is already cooked, arrange on top of casserole after rice is tender and cook for 5 minutes to heat.

Orange Codfish

This will become your favorite way to do fish! Great with Fresh Fruit Salsa, page 95.

Egg whites (large)	2	2
Frozen concentrated unsweetened orange juice, thawed	3 tbsp.	50 mL
Low-sodium soy sauce	2 tbsp.	30 mL
Fine dry bread crumbs	1/2 cup	125 mL
Parsley flakes	1 tsp.	5 mL
Seasoned salt	1/2 tsp.	2 mL
Lemon pepper	1/2 tsp.	2 mL
Fresh (or frozen, thawed) cod fillets	1 lb.	454 g
Canola oil	1 tbsp.	15 mL
Lemon juice	1 tsp.	5 mL

Beat egg whites, orange juice and soy sauce with fork in shallow bowl. Set aside.

Combine next 4 ingredients on sheet of waxed paper.

Dip cod fillets into egg mixture. Coat completely in crumb mixture. Lay in single layer in greased shallow baking dish. Whisk canola oil and lemon juice together in small dish. Drizzle over fish fillets. Bake in 475°F (240°C) oven for 15 to 20 minutes until fish flakes easily. Serves 4.

NUTRITION INFORMATION 1 serving: 217 Calories; 4.9 g Total Fat (0.6 g Sat., 49 mg Cholesterol); 887 mg Sodium; 25 g Protein; 17 g Carbohydrate; trace Dietary Fiber

CHOICES 1 Starch; 3 Protein

Pictured on page 90.

Variation: Omit cod. Use other fish fillets, such as snapper and haddock. Cooking time will be much quicker if very thin fish, such as sole, is used.

To avoid a fish smell in the house after baking any fish, rub the fish with a bit of lemon juice before cooking, then rinse under cold running water. The acid in the juice will change the nitrogen compounds that give off the aroma. Also rinse your hands with lemon juice, then water.

Vegetable Chili

Tastes even better the next day or after being frozen. Keep small portions in the freezer to take for lunch.

Medium onion, chopped	1	1
Garlic cloves, minced (optional)	2	2
Chopped celery	1 cup	250 mL
Canola oil	2 tsp.	10 mL
Large red pepper, chopped	$^1/_2$	$^1/_2$
Large yellow pepper, chopped	$^1/_2$	$^1/_2$
Medium carrots, diced	2	2
Sliced fresh mushrooms	2 cups	500 mL
Diced medium zucchini, with peel	2 cups	500 mL
Can of diced tomatoes, with juice	14 oz.	398 mL
Can of red kidney beans, drained	19 oz.	540 mL
Can of chick peas (garbanzo beans), drained	19 oz.	540 mL
Can of beans in tomato sauce	14 oz.	398 mL
Chopped fresh parsley	$^1/_4$ cup	60 mL
Chili powder	2 tsp.	10 mL
Ground cumin (optional)	$^1/_2$ tsp.	2 mL
Dried whole oregano	$^1/_2$ tsp.	2 mL
Freshly ground pepper, sprinkle		
Dried crushed chilies (optional)	$^1/_8$ tsp.	0.5 mL
Bay leaf	1	1

Freshly ground pepper, for garnish

Sauté onion, garlic and celery in canola oil in heavy-bottomed Dutch oven, stirring occasionally, until very soft.

Add next 16 ingredients. Cover. Simmer for about $1^1/_2$ hours until carrot is tender. Stir occasionally to prevent scorching.

Remove and discard bay leaf. Sprinkle with pepper. Makes 10 cups (2.5 L).

NUTRITION INFORMATION 1 cup (250 mL): 179 Calories; 2.2 g Total Fat (0.2 g Sat., 0 mg Cholesterol); 484 mg Sodium; 9 g Protein; 34 g Carbohydrate; 9 g Dietary Fiber

CHOICES 2 Starch; $^1/_2$ Fruit & Vegetable; 1 Protein

Pictured on page 107.

Although there is no meat in vegetarian dishes, beans and chick peas provide a lot of protein. Kidney beans contain more protein than meat and are very rich in vitamins.

Bean Dumplings In Tomato Sauce

These dumplings provide a filling, nutritious meal with a different taste.

Chopped onion	$^1/_2$ cup	125 mL
Garlic cloves, minced	2	2
Chopped green pepper	$^1/_2$ cup	125 mL
Olive oil	2 tsp.	10 mL
Can of diced tomatoes, with juice	28 oz.	796 mL
Can of tomato juice	10 oz.	284 mL
Granulated sugar	$1^1/_2$ tsp.	7 mL
Chili powder	$^1/_2$ tsp.	2 mL
Hot pepper sauce	$^1/_4$ tsp.	1 mL
All-purpose flour	$^2/_3$ cup	150 mL
Whole wheat flour	$^2/_3$ cup	150 mL
Baking powder	1 tbsp.	15 mL
Salt	$^1/_4$ tsp.	1 mL
Freshly ground pepper	$^1/_8$ tsp.	0.5 mL
Water	$^1/_2$ cup	125 mL
Can of white kidney beans, drained	19 oz.	540 mL
Canola oil	2 tbsp.	30 mL
Egg whites (large)	2	2
Chopped green onion	$^1/_2$ cup	125 mL
Canola oil	1 tsp.	5 mL

Sauté onion, garlic and green pepper in olive oil in large non-stick frying pan until onion is soft. Add tomato, tomato juice, sugar, chili powder and hot pepper sauce. Bring to a boil. Simmer, uncovered, on medium for 30 minutes, stirring several times, until thickened.

Combine both flours, baking powder, salt and pepper in medium bowl.

Process water, beans, canola oil and egg whites in food processor until almost smooth. Stir in green onion. Add to dry ingredients. Stir just until moistened.

Divide and roll dough into about 50 balls ($^1/_2$ tbsp., 7 mL, each). Brown in canola oil in large non-stick frying pan. Add to sauce. Heat for 5 minutes until hot. Serves 6.

NUTRITION INFORMATION 1 serving: 277 Calories; 8 g Total Fat (0.8 g Sat., 0 mg Cholesterol); 636 mg Sodium; 10 g Protein; 44 g Carbohydrate; 5 g Dietary Fiber

CHOICES 2 Starch; 1 Fruit & Vegetable; 1 Protein; 1 Fat & Oil

Pictured on page 107.

Investing in good non-stick cookware makes it easier to use less oil to keep food from sticking when cooking. Olive and canola oils add taste and are low in saturated fats.

Spicy Rice And Beans

Quick and easy. Spiciness can be tamed if desired by using half the amounts of cumin, coriander and chili powder. Eliminating the jalapeño pepper tames it even more.

Chopped onion	1 cup	250 mL
Garlic cloves, minced	3	3
Chopped celery	$^1/_2$ cup	125 mL
Jalapeño pepper, seeded and finely diced	1	1
Canola oil	1 tbsp.	15 mL
Ground cumin	1 tsp.	5 mL
Ground coriander	1 tsp.	5 mL
Chili powder	2 tsp.	10 mL
Long grain brown rice, uncooked	$1^1/_2$ cups	375 mL
Grated carrot	$^1/_2$ cup	125 mL
Water	$2^3/_4$ cups	675 mL
Vegetable bouillon powder	1 tbsp.	15 mL
Bay leaf	1	1
Can of red kidney (or pinto) beans, drained	14 oz.	398 mL
Chopped tomato	1 cup	250 mL
Kernel corn, fresh or frozen	$^1/_2$ cup	125 mL
Chopped fresh cilantro (optional)	1 tbsp.	15 mL
Chopped fresh parsley (or 2 tsp., 10 mL, flakes)	2 tbsp.	30 mL

Sauté onion, garlic, celery and jalapeño pepper in canola oil in large non-stick frying pan for 3 minutes, stirring occasionally. Add cumin, coriander, chili powder and rice. Cook on medium, stirring occasionally, until golden. Stir in carrot, water, bouillon powder and bay leaf. Cover. Simmer on medium-low for 20 minutes.

Stir in beans, tomato and corn. Cover. Heat for 15 to 20 minutes until liquid is absorbed. Remove and discard bay leaf.

Stir in cilantro and 1 tbsp. (15 mL) parsley. Garnish with remaining parsley. Makes 7 cups (1.75 L).

NUTRITION INFORMATION 1 cup (250 mL): 253 Calories; 4 g Total Fat (0.5 g Sat., 0.2 mg Cholesterol); 356 mg Sodium; 8 g Protein; 48 g Carbohydrate; 5 g Dietary Fiber

CHOICES 3 Starch; $^1/_2$ Fruit & Vegetable; $^1/_2$ Fat & Oil

Pictured on page 107.

Hot peppers contain capsaicin in the seeds and ribs. Removing the seeds and ribs will lower the heat but wear rubber gloves when handling the peppers and avoid touching your eyes. Wash your hands well afterwards.

Roasted Pepper And Tomato Pasta

You can't beat this for easy — and the flavor is sublime!

Medium red peppers, cut into 1 inch (2.5 cm) pieces (about 4 cups, 1 L)	3	3
Medium roma (plum) tomatoes, diced (about 4 cups, 1 L)	8	8
Garlic cloves, halved	8	8
Olive oil	1 tbsp.	15 mL
Granulated sugar, pinch		
Salt	$^1/_4$ tsp.	1 mL
Freshly ground pepper, sprinkle		
Medium bow (or shell) pasta (about 10 oz., 285 g)	3 cups	750 mL
Boiling water	3 qts.	3 L
Salt	1 tbsp.	15 mL
Grated light Parmesan cheese	3 tbsp.	50 mL

Combine red pepper, tomato and garlic in large greased shallow glass casserole or enameled roaster (see Tip, below). Drizzle with olive oil. Toss to coat. Bake in 425°F (220°C) oven for 30 minutes. Mix. Bake for 40 minutes until pepper is soft. Sprinkle with sugar, salt and pepper. Mash slightly with fork.

Cook pasta in water and salt in large uncovered pot or Dutch oven for 10 minutes until tender but firm. Drain.

Toss pasta, tomato mixture and Parmesan cheese. Serves 4.

NUTRITION INFORMATION 1 serving: 384 Calories; 6.2 g Total Fat (1.2 g Sat., 1.9 mg Cholesterol); 283 mg Sodium; 14 g Protein; 70 g Carbohydrate; 6 g Dietary Fiber

CHOICES $3^1/_2$ Starch; 2 Fruit & Vegetable; $^1/_2$ Protein; 1 Fat & Oil

Pictured on page 108.

Don't cook tomatoes in a metal pan as taste can be altered by a reaction of the acid and metal.

Red Chard And Garlic Pasta

A very different combination of flavors, and they go together so well.

Finely chopped onion	**1 cup**	**250 mL**
Garlic cloves, minced	**5**	**5**
Olive oil	**2 tsp.**	**10 mL**
Red chard (1 bunch)	**1 lb.**	**454 g**
Water	**$^1/_4$ cup**	**60 mL**
Vegetable bouillon powder	**1 tsp.**	**5 mL**
Finely diced non-fat, low-sodium ham	**$^1/_2$ cup**	**125 mL**
Balsamic vinegar	**2 tbsp.**	**30 mL**
Seedless red grapes, halved	**30**	**30**
Fettuccine	**12 oz.**	**340 g**
Boiling water	**3 qts.**	**3 L**
Salt	**1 tbsp.**	**15 mL**
Chopped walnuts, toasted	**$^1/_3$ cup**	**75 mL**
Chopped fresh parsley	**$^1/_4$ cup**	**60 mL**

Sauté onion and garlic in olive oil in large non-stick frying pan until onion is soft.

Fold each chard leaf lengthwise along the rib. Cut ribs out. Slice ribs crosswise. Coarsely chop leaves and set aside. Add ribs, water, bouillon powder and ham to onion and garlic. Cover. Heat for 5 minutes until chard ribs are tender. Stir in vinegar and grapes. Keep warm.

Cook pasta in boiling water and salt in large uncovered pot or Dutch oven for 10 minutes. Stir in chard leaves. Cook for 2 to 3 minutes until pasta is tender but firm. Drain. Return to pot.

Add chard ribs mixture. Toss. Garnish with walnuts and parsley. Makes 8 cups (2 L). Serves 6.

NUTRITION INFORMATION 1$^1/_2$ cups (375 mL): 321 Calories; 7.3 g Total Fat (0.8 g Sat., 0.1 mg Cholesterol); 424 mg Sodium; 12 g Protein; 53 g Carbohydrate; 4 g Dietary Fiber

CHOICES 3 Starch; 1 Fruit & Vegetable; $^1/_2$ Protein; 1 Fat & Oil

Pictured on page 108.

To toast nuts or coconut, place in shallow pan. Bake in 350°F (175°C) oven for 5 to 10 minutes, stirring often, until desired doneness.

Florentine Pasta Casserole

Mellow spinach with a hint of nutmeg in a pretty, layered dish.

Elbow macaroni	**1¹/₂ cups**	**375 mL**
Boiling water	**8 cups**	**2 L**
Salt	**2 tsp.**	**10 mL**
Lean ground chicken breast	**8 oz.**	**225 g**
Chopped onion	**¹/₂ cup**	**125 mL**
Garlic clove, minced (optional)	**1**	**1**
Seasoned salt	**¹/₄ tsp.**	**1 mL**
Pepper, sprinkle		
Can of skim evaporated milk	**13¹/₂ oz.**	**385 mL**
Skim milk	**1 cup**	**250 mL**
All-purpose flour	**3 tbsp.**	**50 mL**
Parsley flakes (or 1 tbsp., 15 mL, chopped fresh parsley)	**1 tsp.**	**5 mL**
Dill weed	**¹/₂ tsp.**	**2 mL**
Onion powder	**¹/₄ tsp.**	**1 mL**
Seasoned salt	**¹/₄ tsp.**	**1 mL**
Pepper	**¹/₄ tsp.**	**1 mL**
Frozen chopped spinach, thawed and squeezed dry	**10 oz.**	**300 g**
Grated light sharp Cheddar cheese	**1 cup**	**250 mL**

Cook macaroni in boiling water and salt in large uncovered pot or Dutch oven for 8 minutes. Pasta will still be quite firm. Drain. Rinse under cold water. Set aside.

Sauté chicken, onion and garlic in non-stick frying pan until well-cooked and starting to brown. Sprinkle with first amounts of seasoned salt and pepper.

Whisk both milks gradually into flour in small saucepan until smooth. Heat on medium, stirring occasionally, until boiling and thickened. Stir in next 5 ingredients.

Assemble evenly in lightly sprayed 8 cup (2 L) casserole dish as follows:

1. ¹/₂ cup (125 mL) sauce
2. 1 cup (250 mL) macaroni
3. ¹/₂ of chicken mixture
4. ¹/₂ of spinach
5. ³/₄ cup (175 mL) sauce

(continued on next page)

Repeat layers 2, 3 and 4. Top with remaining macaroni and sauce. Cover. Bake in 400°F (205°C) oven for 30 minutes until bubbling.

Sprinkle cheese on top. Bake, uncovered, for 5 minutes. Serves 4.

NUTRITION INFORMATION 1 serving: 457 Calories; 8 g Total Fat (4.3 g Sat., 55.5 mg Cholesterol); 601 mg Sodium; 39 g Protein; 56 g Carbohydrate; 4 g Dietary Fiber

CHOICES $2^1/_2$ Starch; $^1/_2$ Fruit & Vegetable; 2 Milk; $3^1/_2$ Protein

Creamy Garlic Penne

For garlic lovers only! Nice bite from the cayenne pepper.

Can of skim evaporated milk	$13^1/_2$ oz.	385 mL
Skim milk	$1^1/_3$ cups	325 mL
All-purpose flour	3 tbsp.	50 mL
Garlic cloves, minced	2-4	2-4
Vegetable bouillon powder	2 tsp.	10 mL
Boneless, skinless chicken breast halves (about 3), cut into bite-size pieces	$^3/_4$ lb.	340 g
Olive oil	2 tsp.	10 mL
Cayenne pepper	$^1/_2$ tsp.	2 mL
Coarsely ground pepper	$^1/_4$ tsp.	1 mL
Chopped fresh tomato	1 cup	250 mL
Imitation crabmeat (or cooked shrimp), about 6 oz. (170 g)	$1^1/_2$ cups	375 mL
Penne pasta (10 oz., 285 g)	3 cups	750 mL
Boiling water	2 qts.	2 L
Salt (optional)	1 tbsp.	15 mL
Grated light Parmesan cheese (optional)	2 tbsp.	30 mL
Chopped fresh parsley (optional)		

Whisk both milks into flour in large non-stick frying pan until smooth. Add garlic and bouillon powder. Heat and stir on medium-low until boiling and thickened. Keep warm on low, stirring occasionally.

Sauté chicken in olive oil in non-stick frying pan for 5 minutes until slightly browned. Sprinkle with cayenne and pepper. Add tomato and crabmeat. Toss well until hot. Add to garlic sauce. Stir. Keep warm.

Cook pasta in boiling water and salt in large pot or Dutch oven for 10 to 12 minutes until just tender. Drain.

Turn pasta into serving dish. Pour sauce over top. Toss to coat. Sprinkle with Parmesan cheese and parsley. Makes $7^1/_2$ cups (1.9 L). Serves 6.

NUTRITION INFORMATION 1 serving: 379 Calories; 3.9 g Total Fat (0.8 g Sat., 46.7 mg Cholesterol); 549 mg Sodium; 31 g Protein; 54 g Carbohydrate; 2 g Dietary Fiber

CHOICES 3 Starch; $1^1/_2$ Milk; 3 Protein

Pictured on page 108.

Tomato Vegetable Sauce

Serve on pasta as is or freeze in batches and then use in Chicken Chili, page 84, Creamy Pasta Sauce, page 109, Cheese Spirals, page 130, or Minestrone Soup, page 145.

Chopped onion	2 cups	500 mL
Garlic cloves, minced	6	6
Olive oil	1 tbsp.	15 mL
Cans of diced tomatoes (28 oz., 796 mL, each), with juice	3	3
Can of tomato paste	5½ oz.	156 mL
Zucchini, quartered lengthwise and sliced	4 cups	1 L
Medium green, red or yellow peppers, chopped	3	3
Dried sweet basil	2 tsp.	10 mL
Dried whole oregano	2 tsp.	10 mL
Parsley flakes	2 tsp.	10 mL
Coarsely ground pepper	½ tsp.	2 mL
Bay leaf	1	1
Granulated sugar	1 tsp.	5 mL

Sauté onion and garlic in olive oil in large non-stick frying pan, stirring frequently, until onion is golden. Turn into 4 quart (4 L) casserole or small roaster.

Stir in remaining 10 ingredients. Bake, uncovered, in 350°F (175°C) oven for 3 hours, stirring occasionally, until slightly thickened. Remove and discard bay leaf. Mash mixture slightly. Makes 12 cups (3 L). Divide into four 3 cup (750 mL) freezer containers. Label. Freeze.

NUTRITION INFORMATION ½ cup (125 mL): 45 Calories; 1 g Total Fat (0.1 g Sat., 0 mg Cholesterol); 171 mg Sodium; 2 g Protein; 9 g Carbohydrate; 2 g Dietary Fiber

CHOICES 1 Fruit & Vegetable

1. Bean Dumplings In Tomato Sauce, page 100
2. Vegetable Chili, page 99
3. Spicy Rice And Beans, page 101

Creamy Pasta Sauce

Serve this garlicy sauce on your favorite pasta.

Garlic cloves, minced	**4**	**4**
Olive oil	**2 tsp.**	**10 mL**
Can of skim evaporated milk	**13¹/₂ oz.**	**385 mL**
All-purpose flour	**2 tbsp.**	**30 mL**
Container of Tomato Vegetable Sauce (3 cups, 750 mL), page 106, thawed	**1**	**1**
Dried sweet basil	**¹/₂ tsp.**	**2 mL**
Dried whole oregano	**¹/₂ tsp.**	**2 mL**
Salt	**¹/₄ tsp.**	**1 mL**
Pepper	**¹/₈ tsp.**	**0.5 mL**

Sauté garlic in olive oil in medium saucepan until soft.

Whisk skim evaporated milk into flour in small bowl. Add to saucepan. Heat, stirring constantly, until boiling and thickened.

Add sauce, basil and oregano. Heat and stir until heated through. Add salt and pepper. Stir. Makes 4 cups (1 L).

NUTRITION INFORMATION ¹/₂ cup (125 mL): 95 Calories; 2.1 g Total Fat (0.3 g Sat., 1.9 mg Cholesterol); 273 mg Sodium; 6 g Protein; 15 g Carbohydrate; 2 g Dietary Fiber

CHOICES 1 Fruit & Vegetable; 1 Milk; ¹/₂ Fat & Oil

Variation: For a smooth sauce, purée in blender to desired consistency.

1. Creamy Garlic Penne, page 105
2. Roasted Pepper And Tomato Pasta, page 102
3. Red Chard And Garlic Pasta, page 103

Pad Thai

A delicious traditional stir-fry recipe from Thailand. Have all vegetables cut, noodles softened and sauce made before stir-frying.

SAUCE

Fish sauce (available in Asian section of grocery store)	**3 tbsp.**	**50 mL**
Water	**$^1/_2$ cup**	**125 mL**
Chili sauce	**$^1/_3$ cup**	**75 mL**
Brown sugar, packed	**2 tbsp.**	**30 mL**
Low-sodium soy sauce	**$^1/_3$ cup**	**75 mL**
Cornstarch	**4 tsp.**	**20 mL**
Dried crushed chilies (optional)	**$^1/_4$ tsp.**	**1 mL**
Rice vermicelli, broken	**8 oz.**	**225 g**
Cold water, to cover		
Canola oil	**2 tsp.**	**10 mL**
Lean boneless pork loin (or beef sirloin), cut julienne (see Note)	**6 oz.**	**170 g**
Garlic cloves, minced	**2**	**2**
Shredded cabbage	**2 cups**	**500 mL**
Medium carrots, shaved into long, thin ribbons	**2**	**2**
Canola oil	**1 tsp.**	**5 mL**
Egg whites (large), fork-beaten	**2**	**2**
Canola oil	**1 tsp.**	**5 mL**
Fresh bean sprouts	**$^1/_2$ cup**	**125 mL**
Green onions, cut julienne into 4 inch (10 cm) lengths	**3**	**3**
Chopped fresh parsley (or cilantro)	**2 tbsp.**	**30 mL**

Sauce: Combine first 7 ingredients in small bowl. Set aside.

Cover vermicelli with water in large bowl. Let stand for 5 minutes. Drain well. Set aside.

Heat first amount of canola oil in large non-stick frying pan or wok on medium-high. Stir-fry pork and garlic for 1 minute. Add cabbage and carrot. Stir-fry for 4 to 5 minutes until no pink remains in pork and vegetables are tender-crisp. Remove to bowl.

Heat second amount of canola oil in same frying pan. Pour in egg white. Heat, turning once, until firm. Remove to cutting surface. Slice into long shreds. Add to pork and vegetables.

(continued on next page)

Heat third amount of canola oil in same frying pan. Stir-fry bean sprouts, green onion and parsley on medium-high for about 1 minute. Add noodles. Toss. Stir sauce in bowl. Add to vegetable mixture. Heat and stir until boiling and slightly thickened. Add pork mixture. Toss until hot. Makes 11 cups (2.75 L). Serves 6.

NUTRITION INFORMATION 1 serving: 298 Calories; 4.3 g Total Fat (0.5 g Sat., 16 mg Cholesterol); 1307 mg Sodium; 14 g Protein; 52 g Carbohydrate; 3 g Dietary Fiber

CHOICES 2$\frac{1}{2}$ Starch; 1 Fruit & Vegetable; $\frac{1}{2}$ Sugar; 1 Protein

Pictured on page 72.

Note: It is easier to cut pork into thin strips if slightly frozen.

Indonesian Pork Dinner

Lots of color and texture to match the variety of flavors in this dish.

Water	**3$\frac{2}{3}$ cups**	**900 mL**
Vegetable (or chicken) bouillon powder	**1 tbsp.**	**15 mL**
Dried crushed chilies, crushed	**$\frac{1}{4}$ tsp.**	**1 mL**
Long grain brown rice	**1$\frac{1}{2}$ cups**	**375 mL**
Chopped onion	**1 cup**	**250 mL**
Chopped celery	**1 cup**	**250 mL**
Canola oil	**2 tsp.**	**10 mL**
Garlic cloves, minced	**2**	**2**
Grated gingerroot	**2 tsp.**	**10 mL**
Boneless pork loin chops, trimmed and diced	**1 lb.**	**454 g**
Ground cumin	**$\frac{1}{2}$ tsp.**	**2 mL**
Curry powder	**1 tsp.**	**5 mL**
Diced red pepper	**$\frac{1}{4}$ cup**	**60 mL**
Diced yellow pepper	**$\frac{2}{3}$ cup**	**150 mL**
Frozen mixed vegetables, thawed	**$\frac{3}{4}$ cup**	**175 mL**
Shredded cabbage	**2 cups**	**500 mL**
Low-sodium soy sauce	**1$\frac{1}{2}$ tbsp.**	**25 mL**

Combine water, bouillon and dried chilies in large saucepan. Bring to a boil. Stir in rice. Cover. Simmer for 60 to 65 minutes until water is absorbed and rice is tender.

Sauté onion, celery and canola oil in large non-stick frying pan or wok on medium for 2 minutes.

Add next 5 ingredients. Stir-fry for 3 to 4 minutes until no pink remains in pork.

Stir in remaining 5 ingredients. Stir-fry for 3 to 4 minutes until cabbage is softened. Add rice. Toss until rice is steaming hot. Makes 10 cups (2.5 L). Serves 6.

NUTRITION INFORMATION 1 serving: 355 Calories; 8 g Total Fat (2 g Sat., 44.4 mg Cholesterol); 566 mg Sodium; 23 g Protein; 48 g Carbohydrate; 3 g Dietary Fiber

CHOICES 2$\frac{1}{2}$ Starch; 1 Fruit & Vegetable; 2$\frac{1}{2}$ Protein

Fruit-Stuffed Pork Loin

Definitely a company dish. The mixed fruit filling complements the pork very well.

Lean boneless pork tenderloin, trimmed (about 8 × 4 × 2 inch, 20 × 10 × 5 cm, size)	**2$\frac{1}{4}$ lbs.**	**1 kg**
Can of unsweetened applesauce	**14 oz.**	**398 mL**
Garlic cloves, minced	**3**	**3**
Salt	**$\frac{1}{4}$ tsp.**	**1 mL**
Brown sugar, packed	**2 tbsp.**	**30 mL**
Ground cinnamon	**$\frac{1}{8}$ tsp.**	**0.5 mL**
Ground nutmeg	**$\frac{1}{16}$ tsp.**	**0.5 mL**
Boiling water	**2 cups**	**500 mL**
Mixed dried fruit (such as apricots, prunes and cranberries), diced	**1 cup**	**250 mL**
Canola oil	**2 tsp.**	**10 mL**
Dried mixed herbs	**1 tbsp.**	**15 mL**
Garlic clove, minced (optional)	**1**	**1**
Freshly ground pepper, generous sprinkle		
White wine (or apple juice), optional	**$\frac{1}{4}$ cup**	**60 mL**
SAUCE		
Cornstarch	**2 tbsp.**	**30 mL**
Sherry (or non-alcohol sherry)	**$\frac{1}{4}$ cup**	**60 mL**
Ground cinnamon	**$\frac{1}{2}$ tsp.**	**2 mL**
Pepper, sprinkle		

Butterfly tenderloin by cutting horizontally lengthwise, not quite through center. Open flat. Pound with mallet or rolling pin to an even thickness.

Combine $\frac{1}{3}$ cup (75 mL) applesauce with garlic and salt in small bowl. Spread on cut side of pork. Set aside remaining applesauce.

Combine sugar, cinnamon, nutmeg and boiling water in medium bowl. Add dried fruit. Soak for 10 minutes. Drain, reserving liquid. Pack fruit onto pork in even layer, leaving about 1 inch (2.5 cm) from edges on all 4 sides uncovered. Roll jelly roll fashion. Tie with butcher's string or use metal skewers to secure.

Combine canola oil, herbs, garlic, pepper and 1 tbsp. (15 mL) reserved applesauce in small dish. Coat pork. Place on rack in small roaster or pan with sides. Add white wine to bottom of roaster. Cover. Bake in 325°F (160°C) oven for about 1$\frac{1}{4}$ hours until internal temperature reaches 160°F (75°C). Remove from oven. Tent with foil.

(continued on next page)

Sauce: Combine cornstarch and reserved liquid in small saucepan. Add remaining applesauce (about 1¼ cups, 300 mL) and sherry. Heat and stir on medium until boiling and thickened. Makes about 2⅔ cups (650 mL) sauce.

Remove foil from roast. Place on serving platter. Drizzle on sauce. Sprinkle with cinnamon and pepper. Serves 8.

NUTRITION INFORMATION 1 serving: 288 Calories; 8.7 g Total Fat (2.7 g Sat., 74.6 mg Cholesterol); 169 mg Sodium; 29 g Protein; 22 g Carbohydrate; 3 g Dietary Fiber

CHOICES 2 Fruit & Vegetable; 4 Protein

Pictured on page 72.

Pineapple Pork

Good flavor with a touch of sweetness in the peppers and pineapple. Delicious over brown rice.

Lean boneless pork loin, trimmed and thinly sliced	¾ lb.	340 g
Canola oil	2 tsp.	10 mL
Paprika	½ tsp.	2 mL
Ground ginger	½ tsp.	2 mL
Freshly ground pepper, sprinkle		
Medium carrots, thinly sliced on diagonal	2	2
Medium green pepper, cut into large slivers	½	½
Medium red pepper, cut into large slivers	½	½
Small onion, sliced lengthwise into wedges	1	1
Can of pineapple tidbits, juice reserved	14 oz.	398 mL
White vinegar	2 tbsp.	30 mL
Brown sugar, packed	1 tbsp.	15 mL
Reserved pineapple juice	¼ cup	60 mL
Low-sodium soy sauce	1 tbsp.	15 mL
Ketchup	1 tbsp.	15 mL
Cornstarch	2 tbsp.	30 mL

Sauté pork in canola oil in large frying pan for 1 minute. Sprinkle with paprika, ginger and pepper. Sauté until no pink remains in pork.

Stir in next 4 ingredients.

Reserve ¼ cup (60 mL) pineapple juice. Set aside. Add remaining juice and pineapple to pork mixture. Drizzle with vinegar. Sprinkle with brown sugar. Stir. Bring to a boil. Cover. Simmer for 30 minutes until carrot is tender.

Combine reserved juice, soy sauce, ketchup and cornstarch in small bowl until smooth. Stir into pork mixture. Heat and stir until boiling and thickened. Makes 5¼ cups (1.3 L). Serves 4.

NUTRITION INFORMATION 1 serving: 274 Calories; 7.5 g Total Fat (1.9 g Sat., 49.7 mg Cholesterol); 279 mg Sodium; 20 g Protein; 32 g Carbohydrate; 3 g Dietary Fiber

CHOICES 3 Fruit & Vegetable; 2½ Protein

Turkey Breast With Rice Stuffing

So elegant to serve for special guests. Lots of tasty vegetables in the stuffing.

STUFFING

Long grain brown rice	$1/_3$ cup	75 mL
Wild rice	$1/_3$ cup	75 mL
Boiling water	$2^1/_3$ cups	575 mL
Chicken bouillon powder	1 tbsp.	15 mL
Large onion, chopped	1	1
Chopped fresh mushrooms	2 cups	500 mL
Margarine	2 tbsp.	30 mL
Coarsely grated carrot	1 cup	250 mL
Diced red pepper	$2/_3$ cup	150 mL
Chopped fresh parsley (or 1 tbsp., 15 mL, flakes)	3 tbsp.	50 mL
Finely chopped fresh sweet basil (or $1/_2$ tsp., 2 mL, dried)	1 tbsp.	15 mL
Freshly grated lemon peel (optional)	1 tsp.	5 mL
Egg white (large)	1	1
Boneless, skinless turkey breast halves (about $2^1/_2$ lbs., 1.1 kg), see Note	2	2
Water	$1/_4$ cup	60 mL
White (or alcohol-free) wine	$1/_4$ cup	60 mL
Bay leaf	1	1
Freshly ground pepper, sprinkle		
Cornstarch (optional)	$1^1/_2$ tsp.	7 mL

Stuffing: Wash brown and wild rice. Stir into boiling water and bouillon powder in medium saucepan. Cover. Simmer for 40 to 50 minutes until wild rice has popped. Set aside.

Sauté onion and mushrooms in margarine in large frying pan for about 5 minutes until mushrooms have released their juices. Add carrot and red pepper. Sauté for 4 to 5 minutes until vegetables are tender.

Stir in parsley, basil and lemon peel. Add rice. Stir in egg white. Makes 4 cups (1 L) stuffing.

Butterfly each turkey breast by cutting horizontally lengthwise, not quite through thickest part. Open flat. Place, 1 at a time, inside heavy plastic bag or between two sheets of plastic wrap. Pound with mallet or rolling pin to an even thickness. Remove. Pack $1/_2$ of stuffing on center of each breast, leaving edges, about $1/_2$ inch (12 mm), uncovered. Starting with shortest side, roll each breast, enclosing stuffing. Tie at 2 inch (5 cm) intervals with butcher's string. Place seam side down in oval roaster.

Pour water and wine on top. Add bay leaf and pepper. Cover. Bake in 350°F (175°C) oven, basting frequently, for $1^1/_2$ to $1^3/_4$ hours until internal temperature reaches 175°F (80°C). Let stand in covered roaster for 10 minutes. Remove and discard bay leaf.

(continued on next page)

Strain juices. Add enough water to equal $^2/_3$ cup (150 mL). Combine with cornstarch in roaster. Heat and stir until boiling and thickened. Makes $^2/_3$ cup (150 mL) sauce. Each roll cuts into 5 slices. Serves 10.

NUTRITION INFORMATION 1 serving: 220 Calories; 3.6 g Total Fat (0.8 g Sat., 70.5 mg Cholesterol); 291 mg Sodium; 30 g Protein; 14 g Carbohydrate; 1 g Dietary Fiber

CHOICES 1 Starch; 4 Protein

Pictured on page 89.

Note: For 1 large roll (instead of 2 smaller ones), ask the butcher to prepare a whole breast. Flatten as in method. Fill with all the stuffing.

Turkey Vegetable Meatloaf

Have you ever seen a pretty meatloaf? Now you have! Excellent cold in a sandwich.

Medium carrot, cut into $^1/_2$ inch (12 mm) pieces	**1**	**1**
Medium red pepper, cut into chunks	**1**	**1**
Green onions, cut into 1 inch (2.5 cm) pieces	**2**	**2**
Celery rib, cut into 1 inch (2.5 cm) pieces	**1**	**1**
Garlic clove (optional)	**1**	**1**
Skim evaporated milk	**$^1/_2$ cup**	**125 mL**
Egg whites (large)	**3**	**3**
Fine dry whole wheat (or white) bread crumbs	**$1^1/_2$ cups**	**375 mL**
Seasoned salt	**1 tsp.**	**5 mL**
Pepper	**$^1/_4$ tsp.**	**1 mL**
Worcestershire sauce	**1 tsp.**	**5 mL**
Lean ground turkey breast	**$1^1/_4$ lbs.**	**560 g**
Can of stewed tomatoes, with juice	**14 oz.**	**398 mL**
Chopped fresh parsley, for garnish		
Red pepper slices, for garnish		

Process first 7 ingredients in food processor or blender until finely chopped. Pour into large bowl.

Add next 5 ingredients. Mix very well. Form into two 8 x 5 inch (20 x 12.5 cm) loaves. Place crosswise in greased or foil-lined 9 x 13 inch (22 x 33 cm) pan.

Process tomatoes with juice until almost puréed. Pour over meatloaves. Bake, uncovered, in 325°F (160°C) oven for $1^1/_2$ hours. Makes 2 loaves.

Garnish with parsley and red pepper slices. Serves 8.

NUTRITION INFORMATION 1 serving: 204 Calories; 1.6 g Total Fat (0.4 g Sat., 44.2 mg Cholesterol); 554 mg Sodium; 23 g Protein; 23 g Carbohydrate; 1 g Dietary Fiber

CHOICES 1 Starch; 1 Fruit & Vegetable; 3 Protein

Pictured on page 89.

Turkey Pot Pie

Great way to use leftover turkey. Double filling recipe and freeze extra for future use.

FILLING		
Water	2$^1/_2$ cups	625 mL
Chicken (or vegetable) bouillon powder	1 tbsp.	15 mL
Diced red potato, with peel	2 cups	500 mL
Chopped celery	1 cup	250 mL
Finely chopped onion	1 cup	250 mL
Dried rosemary, crushed	$^1/_2$ tsp.	2 mL
Dried thyme	$^1/_4$ tsp.	1 mL
Garlic powder (optional)	$^1/_4$ tsp.	1 mL
Freshly ground pepper, sprinkle		
Frozen mixed vegetables	3 cups	750 mL
Chopped cooked lean turkey (about $^3/_4$ lb., 340 g)	2 cups	500 mL
Skim evaporated milk	$^2/_3$ cup	150 mL
All-purpose flour	3 tbsp.	50 mL
CRUST		
All-purpose flour	$^1/_2$ cup	125 mL
Whole wheat flour	$^1/_2$ cup	125 mL
Baking powder	1$^1/_2$ tsp.	7 mL
Salt	$^1/_2$ tsp.	2 mL
Canola oil	2 tbsp.	30 mL
Skim milk	$^1/_2$ cup	125 mL
Skim milk	1 tbsp.	15 mL
Paprika, sprinkle		

Filling: Combine first 9 ingredients in large uncovered saucepan or Dutch oven. Bring to boil. Cover. Reduce heat. Simmer for 10 minutes.

Add frozen vegetables and turkey. Stir. Cover. Simmer for 15 to 20 minutes until potato is tender.

Whisk evaporated milk into flour in small bowl. Add to turkey mixture. Heat and stir until boiling and thickened. Turn into ungreased 9 x 9 inch (22 x 22 cm) glass pan or 2$^1/_2$ quart (2.5 L) shallow casserole.

Crust: Combine first 4 ingredients in medium bowl.

(continued on next page)

Add canola oil and skim milk all at once. Stir just until moistened. Turn out onto floured surface. Knead gently 8 to 10 times. Roll out $^2/_3$ of dough to $^1/_8$ inch (3 mm) thickness. Cut into $^3/_4$ to 1 inch (2 to 2.5 cm) wide strips. Lay strips, 1 inch (2.5 cm) apart, diagonally on casserole one way. Roll out scraps and remaining dough. Cut strips as above. Lay on casserole diagonally the other way, creating lattice top.

Brush strips with milk. Sprinkle with paprika. Bake, uncovered, in 400°F (205°C) oven for 15 to 20 minutes until bubbling and top is golden brown. Serves 6.

NUTRITION INFORMATION 1 serving: 369 Calories; 7.4 g Total Fat (1.1 g Sat., 57.3 mg Cholesterol); 710 mg Sodium; 28 g Protein; 49 g Carbohydrate; 3 g Dietary Fiber

CHOICES 2 Starch; 2 Fruit & Vegetable; 2½ Protein

Turkey Cutlets With Mushroom Sauce

Ready in 20 minutes. Serve with rice or noodles.

All-purpose flour	$^1/_4$ cup	60 mL
No-salt herb seasoning (such as Mrs. Dash)	1 tbsp.	15 mL
Freshly ground pepper	$^1/_2$ tsp.	2 mL
Turkey breast cutlets, cut into 4 serving-size portions	1 lb.	454 g
Canola oil	2 tsp.	10 mL
Finely chopped onion	$^1/_4$ cup	60 mL
Sliced fresh mushrooms	1$^1/_2$ cups	375 mL
White (or alcohol-free) wine (or chicken broth)	$^1/_2$ cup	125 mL
Skim evaporated milk	$^1/_2$ cup	125 mL
Cornstarch	2 tsp.	10 mL
Chopped fresh parsley (or $^1/_2$ tsp., 2 mL, flakes)	1 tbsp.	15 mL
Salt	$^1/_4$ tsp.	1 mL

Combine flour, herb seasoning and pepper in small dish. Pour onto waxed paper. Coat both sides of cutlets.

Heat canola oil in large non-stick fry pan on medium-high. Quickly brown both sides of cutlets. Remove to plate.

Sauté onion and mushrooms in same pan on medium, stirring occasionally, until mushroom liquid has evaporated and onion and mushrooms are golden and soft. Add wine. Add cutlets and any accumulated juices from the plate. Cover. Simmer for 5 minutes.

Combine remaining 4 ingredients in small dish. Add to liquid in pan. Heat and stir for 1 minute until boiling and thickened. Serves 4.

NUTRITION INFORMATION 1 serving: 246 Calories; 3.4 g Total Fat (0.5 g Sat., 71.6 mg Cholesterol); 268 mg Sodium; 32 g Protein; 15 g Carbohydrate; 1 g Dietary Fiber

CHOICES $^1/_2$ Starch; 1 Milk; 4 Protein

Salads

add some spice to your salad — keep your mouth watering and taste buds guessing. Salads don't have to mean the same old mix of lettuce and tomatoes — this section highlights several variations to help you get your greens — and all the other fresh colors too!

Artichoke Salad

Make the first part of this salad up to 2 days ahead. Just spoon over salad greens when ready to serve.

Medium tomato, cut into 8 wedges	1	1
English cucumber slices, with peel	8	8
Medium ripe olives, cut in half	8	8
Can of artichoke hearts, drained and cut into quarters	14 oz.	398 mL
Medium green pepper, thinly sliced	$^1/_2$	$^1/_2$
Small red onion, thinly sliced (about $^3/_4$ cup, 175 mL)	$^1/_2$	$^1/_2$
Olive oil	2 tbsp.	30 mL
Lemon juice	1 tbsp.	15 mL
White wine vinegar	$1^1/_2$ tsp.	7 mL
Liquid honey	$1^1/_2$ tsp.	7 mL
Garlic clove, minced	1	1
Dried whole oregano	$^1/_4$ tsp.	1 mL
Freshly ground pepper, sprinkle		
Mixed salad greens	6 cups	1.5 L
Crumbled feta cheese, optional	$^1/_4$ cup	60 mL

Combine first 6 ingredients in medium bowl.

Whisk next 7 ingredients together in small bowl. Pour onto vegetables. Gently toss. Chill for at least 1 hour to blend flavors.

Arrange on bed of salad greens. Sprinkle with cheese. Serves 4.

NUTRITION INFORMATION 1 serving: 138 Calories; 8.3 g Total Fat (1.1 g Sat., 0 mg Cholesterol); 280 mg Sodium; 4 g Protein; 15 g Carbohydrate; 5 g Dietary Fiber

CHOICES $1^1/_2$ Fruit & Vegetable; $^1/_2$ Protein; $1^1/_2$ Fat & Oil

Pictured on page 125.

Vinaigrette Potato Salad

Double or triple the recipe to serve a crowd.

Unpeeled baby potatoes	1 lb.	454 g
Water		
Medium carrot, coarsely grated	1	1
Coarsely chopped red pepper	1 cup	250 mL
Green onions, sliced	2	2
DRESSING		
Vegetable bouillon powder	1 tsp.	5 mL
Hot water	$^1/_4$ **cup**	60 mL
Olive oil	2 tbsp.	30 mL
Balsamic vinegar	1 tbsp.	15 mL
Lemon juice	1 tbsp.	15 mL
Garlic clove	1	1
Chopped fresh parsley (or 1 tsp., 5 mL, flakes)	1 tbsp.	15 mL
Chopped fresh marjoram leaves (or 1 tsp., 5 mL, dried)	1 tbsp.	15 mL
Dijon mustard	1 tsp.	5 mL
Salt	$^1/_2$ **tsp.**	2 mL
Freshly ground pepper, sprinkle		

Cook potatoes in water in small saucepan until tender. Drain. Cool. Cut into quarters, or in halves if very small. Place in medium bowl.

Add next 3 ingredients to bowl.

Dressing: Dissolve bouillon powder in hot water in blender. Add remaining 9 ingredients. Process. Pour over salad. Toss. Chill. Toss before serving. Makes 4 cups (1 L).

NUTRITION INFORMATION 1 cup (250 mL): 169 Calories; 7.3 g Total Fat (1 g Sat., 0.1 mg Cholesterol); 524 mg Sodium; 3 g Protein; 24 g Carbohydrate; 3 g Dietary Fiber

CHOICES 1 Starch; 1 Fruit & Vegetable; $1^1/_2$ Fat & Oil

Pictured on front cover and on page 125.

There is no need to cover potatoes with water while boiling. To cook potatoes without losing their nutrients, add $^1/_2$ to 1 inch (1.2 to 2.5 cm) water to the pot. Cover. Bring to a boil. Reduce heat. Simmer until desired doneness.

Couscous Seafood Salad

Slightly chewy with just enough dressing to flavor.

Couscous	¹/₂ **cup**	125 mL
Boiling water	²/₃ **cup**	150 mL
Finely diced green pepper	¹/₂ **cup**	125 mL
Finely diced celery	¹/₄ **cup**	60 mL
Thinly sliced green onion	2 **tbsp.**	30 mL
Chopped imitation crabmeat (about 3 oz., 85 g)	³/₄ **cup**	175 mL
Frozen tiny peas, thawed	¹/₂ **cup**	125 mL
Shredded fresh spinach leaves	³/₄ **cup**	175 mL
Toasted sesame seeds	2 **tsp.**	10 mL
DRESSING		
Rice vinegar	2 **tbsp.**	30 mL
Ketchup	2 **tsp.**	10 mL
Granulated sugar	¹/₂ **tsp.**	2 mL
Garlic powder	¹/₈ **tsp.**	0.5 mL
Ground coriander	¹/₁₆ **tsp.**	0.5 mL
Ground oregano	¹/₁₆ **tsp.**	0.5 mL
Canola oil	1 **tsp.**	5 mL

Stir couscous into boiling water. Cover. Let stand for 5 minutes. Fluff with fork. Turn into medium bowl. Cool.

Add next 7 ingredients. Toss.

Dressing: Whisk all 7 ingredients in small bowl. Pour over spinach mixture. Toss lightly. Makes 4 cups (1 L). Serves 4.

NUTRITION INFORMATION 1 cup (250 mL): 161 Calories; 2.5 g Total Fat (0.4 g Sat., 7.7 mg Cholesterol); 225 mg Sodium; 8 g Protein; 27 g Carbohydrate; 3 g Dietary Fiber

CHOICES 1 Starch; 1 Fruit & Vegetable; ¹/₂ Protein

Marinated Salad

You'll love the refreshing combination of the vegetables and marinade. So easy to make ahead. The bulgur makes it chewy.

Bulgur wheat	¹/₂ **cup**	125 mL
Boiling water	1¹/₂ **cups**	375 mL

(continued on next page)

Seeded, diced tomato	2 cups	500 mL
Diced English cucumber, with peel	2 cups	500 mL
Diced green pepper	1 cup	250 mL
Sliced ripe olives	$1/2$ cup	125 mL
Thinly sliced green onion	$1/4$ cup	60 mL
Feta cheese, crumbled into small pieces, optional	$3/4$ cup	175 mL
Olive oil	2 tbsp.	30 mL
Lemon juice	2 tbsp.	30 mL
Dried whole oregano, crushed	$1/4$ tsp.	1 mL
Salt	$1/4$ tsp.	1 mL
Freshly ground pepper, to taste		
Torn romaine lettuce	6 cups	1.5 L

Soak bulgur in boiling water in small saucepan for 10 minutes. Drain. Set aside.

Combine next 11 ingredients in large bowl. Cover. Let stand at room temperature for 30 minutes. Drain and discard liquid. Add bulgur.

Add lettuce. Toss gently. Serve immediately. Serves 8.

NUTRITION INFORMATION 1 serving: 70 Calories; 1.9 g Total Fat (0.,3 g Sat., 0 mg Cholesterol); 142 mg Sodium; 3 g Protein; 12 g Carbohydrate; 4 g Dietary Fiber

CHOICES $1/2$ Starch; $1/2$ Fruit & Vegetable; $1/2$ Fat & Oil

Pictured on front cover.

Caesar Salad Dressing

You'll never miss the eggs and oil in this tasty substitute for high-fat Caesar dressing.

Garlic clove(s)	1-2	1-2
Water	1 tbsp.	15 mL
Lemon juice	1 tbsp.	15 mL
Red wine vinegar	1 tbsp.	15 mL
Dry mustard	$1/4$ tsp.	1 mL
Silken (or soft) tofu	$3/4$ cup	175 mL
Anchovy paste	1 tbsp.	15 mL
Salt	$1/8$ tsp.	0.5 mL
Freshly ground pepper, sprinkle		
Grated light Parmesan cheese	1 tbsp.	15 mL

Process all 10 ingredients in blender until smooth. Makes 1 cup (250 mL).

NUTRITION INFORMATION 2 tbsp. (30 mL): 27 Calories; 1.5 g Total Fat (0.3 g Sat., 2.4 mg Cholesterol); 150 mg Sodium; 3 g Protein; 1 g Carbohydrate; trace Dietary Fiber

CHOICES $1/2$ Protein

Bows Salad

This luncheon salad keeps very well for up to three days in the refrigerator.

Large yellow pepper	1	1
Medium bow pasta	8 oz.	225 g
Boiling water	2 qts.	2 L
Salt	2 tsp.	10 mL
DRESSING		
Low-fat mayonnaise	$^1/_3$ **cup**	75 mL
Non-fat sour cream	$^1/_4$ **cup**	60 mL
Low-sodium soy sauce	2 tsp.	10 mL
Paprika	1 tsp.	5 mL
Hot pepper sauce	$^1/_8$ **tsp.**	0.5 mL
Granulated sugar, pinch		
Can of white tuna, packed in water, undrained	6 oz.	170 g
Seeded, diced tomato	2 cups	500 mL
Green onions, thinly sliced	2	2

Roast pepper on baking sheet under broiler, turning frequently, until skin is blistered and blackened. Place in small bowl. Cover with plastic wrap for 15 minutes. Peel and discard blackened skin. Remove seeds and membrane. Strain juice into small bowl and reserve. Cut pepper into slivers.

Cook pasta in boiling water and salt in large uncovered pot or Dutch oven for 10 to 12 minutes until tender but firm. Drain. Rinse with cold water.

Dressing: Combine mayonnaise, sour cream, soy sauce, paprika and hot pepper sauce in medium bowl until smooth. Add sugar and reserved pepper juice. Add tuna with water. Stir, breaking up tuna with fork.

Combine tomato and green onion in large bowl. Add pepper, pasta and dressing. Toss gently to coat. Cover. Chill well before serving. Makes about 4 cups (1 L).

NUTRITION INFORMATION 1 cup (250 mL): 349 Calories; 8.5 g Total Fat (0.8 g Sat., 15 mg Cholesterol); 453 mg Sodium; 18 g Protein; 50 g Carbohydrate; 3 g Dietary Fiber

CHOICES 3 Starch; $^1/_2$ Fruit & Vegetable; $1^1/_2$ Protein; 1 Fat & Oil

Quick Pasta Salad

Using canned peppers and enhancing bottled dressing makes this fast to prepare.

Rotini pasta	2 cups	500 mL
Boiling water	2 qts.	2 L
Salt	2 tsp.	10 mL
Can of roasted red peppers, drained and cut into 2 inch (5 cm) slivers	14 oz.	398 mL
Paper-thin sliced red onion	1 cup	250 mL

(continued on next page)

Non-fat French dressing	¹/₂ cup	125 mL
Garlic clove(s), minced	1-2	1-2
Dried whole oregano, crushed	¹/₄ tsp.	1 mL
Freshly ground pepper, sprinkle		

Cook pasta in boiling water and salt in large uncovered saucepan for 10 to 12 minutes until tender but firm. Drain. Rinse well with cold water. Drain.

Combine pasta with pepper and onion in medium bowl.

Combine remaining 4 ingredients in small bowl. Pour over salad. Mix well. Cover. Chill. Serves 4.

NUTRITION INFORMATION 1 serving: 248 Calories; 0.9 g Total Fat (0.1 g Sat., 0 mg Cholesterol); 444 mg Sodium; 8 g Protein; 52 g Carbohydrate; 3 g Dietary Fiber

CHOICES 2 Starch; 1 Fruit & Vegetable; 1 Sugar

Mediterranean Garbanzo Salad

All the flavors come together in a full and rich taste once salad has chilled.

Can of garbanzo beans (chick peas), drained	19 oz.	540 g
Diced English cucumber, with peel	1 cup	250 mL
Medium roma (plum) tomatoes, seeded and diced (1¹/₃ cups, 325 mL)	3	3
Finely chopped red onion	¹/₄ cup	60 mL
Diced green pepper	¹/₂ cup	125 mL
Sliced ripe olives	¹/₄ cup	60 mL
FETA CHEESE DRESSING		
1% buttermilk	2 tbsp.	30 mL
Olive oil	1 tsp.	5 mL
Chopped fresh oregano leaves (or 1 tsp., 5 mL, dried)	2 tsp.	10 mL
Chopped fresh parsley (or 2 tsp., 10 mL, flakes)	1 tbsp.	15 mL
Light feta cheese, crumbled	¹/₂ cup	125 mL
Freshly ground pepper, sprinkle		
Grated lemon peel (or juice)	1 tsp.	5 mL
Garlic clove(s), minced (or ¹/₄ tsp., 1 mL, powder)	1-2	1-2

Combine first 6 ingredients in large bowl. Makes 6 cups (1.5 L) vegetables.

Feta Cheese Dressing: Process all 8 ingredients in blender until quite smooth. Makes ²/₃ cup (150 mL) dressing. Add to vegetables. Toss to coat. Chill for at least 1 to 2 hours to blend flavors. Serves 8.

NUTRITION INFORMATION 1 serving: 99 Calories; 3.8 g Total Fat (1.6 g Sat., 8.3 mg Cholesterol); 208 mg Sodium; 5 g Protein; 13 g Carbohydrate; 2 g Dietary Fiber

CHOICES ¹/₂ Starch; ¹/₂ Fruit & Vegetable; ¹/₂ Protein; ¹/₂ Fat & Oil

Pictured on page 125.

Cheese And Artichoke Salad

This keeps well in a covered container in the refrigerator for up to two days. Only 15 minutes preparation time.

DRESSING

Non-fat Italian dressing	$^1/_2$ cup	125 mL
White (or alcohol-free) wine	2 tbsp.	30 mL
Small garlic clove, minced	1	1
Dried rosemary (or pinch of ground rosemary)	$^1/_2$ tsp.	2 mL
Large shell pasta (not jumbo), about 5 oz. (140 g)	$1^3/_4$ cups	425 mL
Boiling water	6 cups	1.5 L
Salt	$1^1/_2$ tsp.	7 mL
Can of artichoke hearts, drained and chopped	14 oz.	398 mL
Part-skim mozzarella cheese, cut into $^1/_2$ inch (12 mm) cubes	4 oz.	113 g
Diced red pepper	$^1/_4$ cup	60 mL

Dressing: Combine dressing, wine, garlic and rosemary in small bowl. Let stand at room temperature for at least 15 minutes.

Cook pasta in boiling water and salt in large saucepan for about 8 minutes until tender but firm. Drain. Rinse with cold water. Drain. Place in medium bowl.

Add artichoke, cheese and red pepper. Add dressing. Toss to coat. Cover. Chill. Makes 5 cups (1.25 L).

NUTRITION INFORMATION 1 cup (250 mL): 200 Calories; 4.3 g Total Fat (2.4 g Sat., 13.5 mg Cholesterol); 536 mg Sodium; 11 g Protein; 29 g Carbohydrate; 3 g Dietary Fiber

CHOICES $1^1/_2$ Starch; $^1/_2$ Fruit & Vegetable; 1 Protein

Fresh Strawberry Dressing

Wonderful strawberry flavor with a nice peppery aftertaste.

Chopped fresh strawberries	**1 cup**	**250 mL**
White wine vinegar	**1 tbsp.**	**15 mL**
Balsamic vinegar	**1^1/$_2$ tsp.**	**7 mL**
Liquid honey (optional)	**1 tsp.**	**5 mL**
Freshly ground pepper	**1 tsp.**	**5 mL**

Process all 5 ingredients in blender until smooth. Makes 1 cup (250 mL).

NUTRITION INFORMATION 2 tbsp. (30 mL): 6 Calories; 0.1 g Total Fat (trace Sat., 0 mg Cholesterol); trace Sodium; trace Protein; 2 g Carbohydrate; trace Dietary Fiber

CHOICES Extra

Pictured on page 125.

Creamy Orange Dressing

Serve this refreshing dressing with spinach or mixed salad greens.

Frozen concentrated orange juice, thawed (half of 12^1/$_2$ oz., 355 mL, can)	**^{3}/$_4$ cup**	**175 mL**
White wine vinegar	**2 tbsp.**	**30 mL**
Non-fat plain yogurt	**^{1}/$_2$ cup**	**125 mL**
Liquid honey (or sugar substitute, such as Sugar Twin, to desired sweetness)	**1 tbsp.**	**15 mL**
Ground cinnamon	**^{1}/$_4$ tsp.**	**1 mL**

Whisk all 5 ingredients in small bowl until smooth. Makes 1^1/$_2$ cups (375 mL).

NUTRITION INFORMATION 2 tbsp. (30 mL): 40 Calories; 0.1 g Total Fat (trace Sat., 0.2 mg Cholesterol); 8 mg Sodium; 1 g Protein; 9 g Carbohydrate; trace Dietary Fiber

CHOICES 1 Fruit & Vegetable

Pictured on page 125.

1. Bulgur Curry, page 132
2. Spicy Potato Bumps, page 131
3. Cheese Spirals, page 130

Side Dishes

Like Watson to Sherlock Holmes, a side dish complements many meals. Whether it's a bowl of potatoes, rice or pasta, all it takes is a few simple ingredients to create these recipes, which will appeal to a wide range of people.

Creamy Garlic Spaghetti

A great side dish with just about any meat.

Box of whole wheat spaghetti	**13 oz.**	**375 g**
Boiling water	**4 qts.**	**4 L**
Salt	**4 tsp.**	**20 mL**
Chopped onion	**1¹/₂ cups**	**375 mL**
Garlic cloves, minced	**6**	**6**
Olive oil	**1 tbsp.**	**15 mL**
All-purpose flour	**1 tbsp.**	**15 mL**
Vegetable (or chicken) bouillon powder	**1 tsp.**	**5 mL**
Water	**³/₄ cup**	**175 mL**
Skim evaporated milk	**¹/₄ cup**	**60 mL**
Grated light Parmesan cheese	**¹/₄ cup**	**60 mL**
Chopped fresh parsley, for garnish		

Cook pasta in boiling water and salt in large uncovered pot or Dutch oven for 8 to 10 minutes until tender but firm. Drain well.

Sauté onion and garlic in olive oil in large non-stick frying pan for about 5 minutes until onion is golden and very soft. Sprinkle with flour and bouillon powder. Mix well. Gradually stir in water and milk. Heat and stir until bubbling. Cover. Simmer for about 30 minutes until thickened. Purée in blender. Makes 1¹/₄ cups (300 mL).

Turn pasta into large bowl. Add sauce and Parmesan cheese. Toss. Garnish with parsley. Makes 6 cups (1.5 L).

NUTRITION INFORMATION 1 cup (250 mL): 287 Calories; 4 g Total Fat (0.9 g Sat., 2.2 mg Cholesterol); 206 mg Sodium; 13 g Protein; 54 g Carbohydrate; 8 g Dietary Fiber

CHOICES 3 Starch; ¹/₂ Fruit & Vegetable; ¹/₂ Protein; ¹/₂ Fat & Oil

Italian Potato Casserole

Moist and tender with herb and pepper aftertaste.

Medium onion, sliced	1	1
Garlic clove, minced	1	1
Olive oil	1 tsp.	5 mL
Skim evaporated milk	1 cup	250 mL
All-purpose flour	3 tbsp.	50 mL
Prepared mustard	2 tsp.	10 mL
Salt	$\frac{1}{2}$ tsp.	2 mL
Dried sweet basil	$\frac{1}{2}$ tsp.	2 mL
Granulated sugar	$\frac{1}{4}$ tsp.	1 mL
Dried whole oregano	$\frac{1}{8}$ tsp.	0.5 mL
Unpeeled medium new potatoes, thinly sliced (about 4 cups, 1 L)	4	4
Freshly ground pepper	$\frac{1}{8}$ tsp.	0.5 mL
Medium roma (plum) tomatoes, sliced $\frac{1}{4}$ inch (6 mm) thick	4	4
Grated light Parmesan cheese	1 tbsp.	15 mL

Sauté onion and garlic in olive oil in medium non-stick frying pan until onion is soft.

Combine evaporated milk and flour in small bowl until smooth. Slowly add to onion, stirring constantly, until boiling and thickened. Stir in mustard, salt, basil, sugar and oregano.

Arrange $\frac{1}{2}$ of potatoes in greased 2 quart (2 L) casserole. Sprinkle with pepper. Layer with $\frac{1}{2}$ of tomato slices. Cover with $\frac{1}{2}$ of onion sauce. Repeat layers. Sprinkle with Parmesan cheese. Cover. Bake in 375°F (190°C) oven for 45 minutes. Remove cover. Bake for 20 to 30 minutes until golden brown and potatoes are soft. Makes 5 cups (1.25 L).

NUTRITION INFORMATION $\frac{3}{4}$ cup (175 mL): 161 Calories; 1.6 g Total Fat (0.3 g Sat., 2 mg Cholesterol); 337 mg Sodium; 8 g Protein; 31 g Carbohydrate; 3 g Dietary Fiber

CHOICES 1 Starch; 1 Fruit & Vegetable; 1 Milk

Pictured on page 143.

Generally, when substituting dried for fresh herbs, use about $\frac{1}{4}$ of the amount requested. For example, you would use 1 tsp. (5 mL) dried where the recipe called for 1 tbsp. (15 mL) of fresh herbs.

Cheese Spirals

Uses a container of Tomato Vegetable Sauce, page 106.

Lasagna noodles	8	8
Boiling water	3 qts.	3 L
Salt	1 tbsp.	15 mL
Grated part-skim mozzarella cheese	$1/2$ cup	125 mL
Part-skim ricotta cheese	$1/2$ cup	125 mL
Grated light Parmesan cheese	2 tbsp.	30 mL
Dried marjoram, crushed	$1/2$ tsp.	2 mL
Dried sweet basil	1 tsp.	5 mL
Egg white (large), fork-beaten	1	1
Container of Tomato Vegetable Sauce (3 cups, 750 mL), page 106, thawed	1	1

Cook noodles in boiling water and salt in large uncovered pot or Dutch oven for 12 to 14 minutes until tender but firm. Drain. Rinse in cold water. Drain.

Combine mozzarella, ricotta and Parmesan cheeses in small bowl. Add marjoram, basil and egg white. Mix. Spread mixture along lengths of 8 cooked noodles. Roll up each, jelly roll style. Place seam side down in shallow baking dish.

Pour sauce over rolls. Cover. Bake in 350°F (175°C) oven for 30 to 40 minutes until bubbling and hot. Makes 8 rolls. Serves 4.

NUTRITION INFORMATION 1 serving: 315 Calories; 7.7 g Total Fat (3.8 g Sat., 20.1 mg Cholesterol); 440 mg Sodium; 17 g Protein; 46 g Carbohydrate; 4 g Dietary Fiber

CHOICES 2 Starch; 1 Fruit & Vegetable; $1^1/2$ Protein; $1/2$ Fat & Oil

Pictured on page 126.

Mashed Garlic Potatoes

Boost the flavor of ordinary mashed potatoes in one easy step!

Potatoes, peeled and cut into large chunks	$1^1/2$ lbs.	680 g
Garlic cloves, cut in half	6	6
Salt	1 tsp.	5 mL
Boiling water		
Skim evaporated milk	$1/3$ cup	75 mL
Freshly ground pepper, sprinkle		

(continued on next page)

Cook potatoes with garlic and salt in boiling water in medium saucepan for 12 minutes until tender. Drain, reserving ¼ cup (60 mL) potato water.

Mash potato, reserved potato water, evaporated milk and pepper until smooth and fluffy. Makes 3½ cups (875 mL). Serves 6.

NUTRITION INFORMATION 1 serving: 106 Calories; 0.2 g Total Fat (0.1 g Sat., 0.5 mg Cholesterol); 25 mg Sodium; 4 g Protein; 23 g Carbohydrate; 2 g Dietary Fiber

CHOICES 1½ Starch

Spicy Potato Bumps

Any combination of spices could be used for these, and they would still be as delicious!

Unpeeled medium baking potatoes	**6**	**6**
Olive oil	**1 tbsp.**	**15 mL**
Parsley flakes	**2 tsp.**	**10 mL**
Salt	**1½ tsp.**	**7 mL**
Chili powder	**1 tsp.**	**5 mL**
Paprika	**1 tsp.**	**5 mL**
Dried thyme, crushed	**½ tsp.**	**2 mL**
Garlic powder	**¼ tsp.**	**1 mL**
Cayenne pepper	**⅛ tsp.**	**0.5 mL**
Ground rosemary	**1/16 tsp.**	**0.5 mL**

Cut each potato in quarters lengthwise. Cut each quarter crosswise into 3 pieces. Toss potato with olive oil in large bowl.

Combine remaining 8 ingredients in small cup. Sprinkle over potato. Toss to coat. Spread on large greased baking sheet with sides. Bake, uncovered, in center of 425°F (220°C) oven. Cook for about 45 minutes, stirring twice, until browned and tender. Serves 6.

NUTRITION INFORMATION 1 serving: 134 Calories; 2.6 g Total Fat (0.4 g Sat., 0 mg Cholesterol); 694 mg Sodium; 3 g Protein; 25 g Carbohydrate; 3 g Dietary Fiber

CHOICES 1½ Starch; ½ Fat & Oil

Pictured on page 126.

Baking potatoes have a drier, fluffier texture which isn't as suitable for salads. They are often older potatoes and have russet-colored skin.

Barley Side Dish

Wonderful barley flavor and chewy texture.

Chopped onion	$^1/_2$ cup	125 mL
Chopped celery	$^1/_2$ cup	125 mL
Canola oil	2 tsp.	10 mL
Pearl barley	1 cup	250 mL
Boiling water	$3^1/_2$ cups	875 mL
Beef bouillon powder	1 tbsp.	15 mL
Medium carrot, grated	1	1
Chopped green onion (or chives)	2 tbsp.	30 mL

Sauté onion and celery in canola oil in large frying pan until soft. Add barley. Sauté for about 10 minutes until barley is toasted. Turn into medium saucepan.

Stir in water, bouillon powder and carrot. Bring to a boil. Reduce heat. Cover. Simmer for 30 to 35 minutes until liquid is absorbed. Stir in green onion. Makes 4 cups (1 L).

NUTRITION INFORMATION $^3/_4$ cup (175 mL): 146 Calories; 2.5 g Total Fat (0.4 g Sat., 0.2 mg Cholesterol); 316 mg Sodium; 5 g Protein; 27 g Carbohydrate; 6 g Dietary Fiber

CHOICES $1^1/_2$ Starch; $^1/_2$ Fruit & Vegetable; $^1/_2$ Fat & Oil

Bulgur Curry

Such a warm, pretty color—and it tastes good too. Makes an impressive buffet dish.

Large onion, chopped	1	1
Chopped fresh mushrooms	1 cup	250 mL
Diced red or green pepper	1 cup	250 mL
Olive oil	2 tsp.	10 mL
Curry paste (available in Asian section of grocery store)	1 tsp.	5 mL
Dark raisins	$^1/_3$ cup	75 mL
Water	3 cups	750 mL
Chicken bouillon powder	1 tbsp.	15 mL
Bulgur wheat	$1^1/_4$ cups	300 mL
Chopped fresh parsley (or 1 tbsp., 15 mL, flakes)	$^1/_4$ cup	60 mL

(continued on next page)

Sauté onion, mushrooms and pepper in olive oil in large saucepan on medium for about 10 minutes until onion is soft and liquid is evaporated.

Stir in curry paste and raisins. Add water, chicken bouillon powder and bulgur. Bring to a boil. Reduce heat. Cover. Simmer for about 20 minutes until liquid is absorbed.

Stir in parsley before serving. Makes 5 cups (1.25 L).

NUTRITION INFORMATION ¹/₂ cup (125 mL): 99 Calories; 1.5 g Total Fat (0.2 g Sat., 0.1 mg Cholesterol); 200 mg Sodium; 3 g Protein; 20 g Carbohydrate; 4 g Dietary Fiber

CHOICES 1 Starch; ¹/₂ Fruit & Vegetable

Pictured on page 126.

Rice Pilaf

Nice toasted grain flavor. Try the variation for even more fiber.

Chopped onion	**¹/₂ cup**	**125 mL**
Sliced fresh mushrooms	**1 cup**	**250 mL**
Canola oil	**2 tsp.**	**10 mL**
Long grain white rice	**¹/₂ cup**	**125 mL**
Bulgur wheat	**¹/₂ cup**	**125 mL**
Can of condensed chicken broth	**10 oz.**	**284 mL**
Water	**³/₄ cup**	**175 mL**
Chopped fresh parsley (optional)	**1 tbsp.**	**15 mL**

Sauté onion and mushrooms in canola oil in large frying pan until soft. Add rice and bulgur. Sauté for about 10 minutes until rice is toasted. Turn into medium saucepan.

Stir in broth and water. Bring to a boil. Reduce heat. Cover. Simmer for 20 minutes until liquid is absorbed.

Stir in parsley. Makes 3 cups (750 mL).

NUTRITION INFORMATION ¹/₂ cup (125 mL): 139 Calories; 2.4 g Total Fat (0.3 g Sat., 0.5 mg Cholesterol); 318 mg Sodium; 5 g Protein; 25 g Carbohydrate; 3 g Dietary Fiber

CHOICES 1¹/₂ Starch; ¹/₂ Fat & Oil

Variation: For more color and fiber, stir in 1 cup (250 mL) hot cooked peas just before serving.

Barley And Rice Pilaf

The barley makes it slightly chewy. Good blend of flavors, but you can add up to a teaspoon (5 mL) of your favorite no-salt herb mix (such as Mrs. Dash) for more of a flavor burst.

Pearl barley	³/₄ cup	175 mL
Long grain brown rice	³/₄ cup	175 mL
Canola oil	1 tbsp.	15 mL
Chopped onion	1 cup	250 mL
Chopped celery rib, with leaves	1 cup	250 mL
Water	3¹/₂ cups	875 mL
Vegetable bouillon powder	1 tbsp.	15 mL
Coarsely grated carrot	¹/₂ cup	125 mL
Diced green pepper	¹/₂ cup	125 mL
Diced red pepper	¹/₂ cup	125 mL
Diced yellow or orange pepper	¹/₂ cup	125 mL
Garlic powder	¹/₄ tsp.	1 mL
Chopped fresh parsley (or 2 tsp., 10 mL, flakes)	3 tbsp.	50 mL
Salt	1¹/₂ tsp.	7 mL
Pepper	¹/₂ tsp.	2 mL

Sauté barley and rice in canola oil in large heavy-bottomed saucepan for about 8 minutes until starting to turn golden brown.

Add onion and celery. Sauté for 3 to 4 minutes until celery is tender-crisp. Add next 3 ingredients. Bring to a boil. Reduce heat. Cover. Simmer for 40 minutes.

Stir in remaining 7 ingredients. Cover. Simmer for 20 to 30 minutes until water is absorbed and barley is tender. Makes 6 cups (1.5 L).

NUTRITION INFORMATION ¹/₂ cup (125 mL): 115 Calories; 2 g Total Fat (0.3 g Sat., 0.1 mg Cholesterol); 502 mg Sodium; 3 g Protein; 22 g Carbohydrate; 3 g Dietary Fiber

CHOICES 1 Starch; ¹/₂ Fruit & Vegetable

Pictured on page 143 and on back cover.

Lentil Rice

Exotic Middle Eastern influences in this tasty dish. Makes a big batch and rewarms wonderfully for lunches at work.

Water	12 cups	3 L
Green lentils	2 cups	500 mL
Bay leaves	5	5
Dried crushed chilies	¹/₄ tsp.	1 mL
Salt	1 tsp.	5 mL
Freshly ground pepper	1 tsp.	5 mL
Long grain white rice	1 cup	250 mL
Pickled hot peppers, chopped (optional)	¹/₂ cup	125 mL

(continued on next page)

• SIDE DISHES •

Combine first 6 ingredients in large 4 quart (4 L) Dutch oven. Cover. Simmer for 40 minutes until lentils are tender but firm.

Stir in rice. Bring to a boil. Cover. Simmer 15 to 20 minutes until rice is tender. Drain any remaining liquid. Stir in chopped hot pepper. Makes 8 cups (2 L).

NUTRITION INFORMATION ¹/₂ cup (125 mL): 131 Calories; 0.3 g Total Fat (0.1 g Sat., 0 mg Cholesterol); 173 mg Sodium; 8 g Protein; 24 g Carbohydrate; 3 g Dietary Fiber

CHOICES 1¹/₂ Starch; 1 Protein

Pictured on page 72.

Creamy Mushroom Risotto

Contains threads of spinach throughout. The continuous stirring is what makes it creamy.

Olive oil	2 tsp.	10 mL
Sliced fresh mushrooms	3 cups	750 mL
Garlic clove, minced	1	1
Dried sweet basil	1¹/₂ tsp.	7 mL
Freshly ground pepper, sprinkle		
Water	1¹/₂ cups	375 mL
Vegetable bouillon powder	1 tbsp.	15 mL
Short grain white (or arborio) rice	1¹/₂ cups	375 mL
Water	1¹/₄ cups	300 mL
White (or alcohol-free) wine	¹/₄ cup	60 mL
Skim milk	¹/₄ cup	60 mL
Chopped fresh spinach leaves, lightly packed, cut chiffonade (see Tip, page 15)	3 cups	750 mL
Chopped toasted pine nuts (or almonds)	¹/₃ cup	75 mL
Freshly grated Parmesan (or Romano) cheese	¹/₄ cup	60 mL

Heat olive oil in large non-stick frying pan. Add mushrooms, garlic, basil and pepper. Heat and stir on medium-high for about 10 minutes until liquid is evaporated and mushrooms are browned.

Add first amount of water, vegetable bouillon powder and rice. Bring to a boil. Heat and stir until most water is absorbed.

Add second amount of water, ¹/₄ cup (60 mL) at a time, while stirring. Allow water to absorb each time more is added.

Add wine. Heat and stir until absorbed. Stir in milk and spinach. Heat and stir until milk is absorbed and spinach is soft. Turn into warm serving bowl. Sprinkle with nuts and cheese. Makes 5 cups (1.25 L).

NUTRITION INFORMATION 1 cup (250 mL): 304 Calories; 8.4 g Total Fat (2 g Sat., 3.9 mg Cholesterol); 412 mg Sodium; 10 g Protein; 47 g Carbohydrate; 3 g Dietary Fiber

CHOICES 3 Starch; ¹/₂ Protein; 1 Fat & Oil

Vegetable Medley

These take 1½ hours to bake. Put in with roast, and everything will be ready at the same time.

Red baby potatoes, halved	1 lb.	454 g
Medium sweet potatoes, cut bite size (about 1 lb., 454 g)	2	2
Parsnips, cut bite size (about 2 cups, 500 mL)	3	3
Carrots, cut bite size (about 2½ cups, 625 mL)	5	5
Chopped onion	⅔ cup	150 mL
Boiling water	3 tbsp.	50 mL
Margarine	1 tsp.	5 mL
Chicken bouillon powder	½ tsp.	2 mL
Garlic clove(s), minced (optional)	1-2	1-2
Parsley flakes	½ tsp.	2 mL
Seasoned salt	½ tsp.	2 mL
Pepper	⅛ tsp.	0.5 mL

Place first 4 ingredients in greased 9 × 13 inch (22 × 33 cm) baking pan or shallow 2 quart (2 L) casserole. Add onion. Stir.

Pour boiling water over margarine and bouillon powder in small bowl. Stir to dissolve. Stir in remaining 4 ingredients. Pour mixture over vegetables. Toss gently. Cover tightly with foil or lid. Bake in 350°F (175°C) oven for 1½ hours until vegetables are tender. Uncover for last 10 to15 minutes to evaporate liquid in pan. Serves 6.

NUTRITION INFORMATION 1 serving: 210 Calories; 1.3 g Total Fat (0.3 g Sat., trace Cholesterol); 218 mg Sodium; 4 g Protein; 47 g Carbohydrate; 7 g Dietary Fiber
CHOICES 2 Starch; 1½ Fruit & Vegetable

Tomatoes Provençale

Make this dish when tomatoes are fresh out of your garden.

Whole wheat bread slices, torn up	2	2
Garlic clove, minced	1	1
Ground rosemary	⅛ tsp.	0.5 mL
Salt	⅛ tsp.	0.5 mL
Freshly ground pepper, generous sprinkle		
Ripe medium round tomatoes	4	4
Olive oil	2 tsp.	10 mL

(continued on next page)

Process bread, garlic, rosemary, salt and pepper in blender or food processor until crumbled.

Cut tomatoes into thick slices. Place in rows, slightly overlapping, in 9 x 13 inch (22 x 33 cm) pan or shallow 2 quart (2 L) baking dish. Brush surface with olive oil. Sprinkle with crumb mixture. Bake, uncovered, in 400°F (205°C) oven for 10 minutes until crumbs are browned and slightly crisp. Serves 6.

NUTRITION INFORMATION 1 serving: 54 Calories; 2 g Total Fat (0.3 g Sat., 0.3 mg Cholesterol); 116 mg Sodium; 2 g Protein; 9 g Carbohydrate; 2 g Dietary Fiber

CHOICES $^1/_2$ Starch

Cold Dressed Asparagus

This is a great make-ahead recipe. It suits an elegant dinner party, an outdoor barbecue or a potluck.

Ripe medium tomato, quartered	1	1
Green onion, cut into 1 inch (2.5 cm) pieces	1	1
Garlic cloves	2	2
Red wine vinegar	3 tbsp.	50 mL
Liquid honey	1 tbsp.	15 mL
Chopped fresh parsley	1 tbsp.	15 mL
Olive oil	1 tbsp.	15 mL
Anchovy paste	2 tsp.	10 mL
Paprika	1 tsp.	5 mL
Salt	$^1/_2$ tsp.	2 mL
Fresh asparagus, trimmed of tough ends	1 lb.	454 g
Very thinly sliced red onion	1$^1/_2$ cups	375 mL
Chopped pitted ripe olives (optional)	2 tbsp.	30 mL

Process first 10 ingredients in blender for about 1 minute until smooth. Chill for 1 hour to blend flavors. Makes 1$^1/_4$ cups (300 mL) dressing.

Steam asparagus for 4 to 5 minutes until tender-crisp. Drain. Rinse in cold water until completely cool. Drain well.

Arrange asparagus on small platter with onion. Scatter with olives. Drizzle dressing over top. Serve chilled or at room temperature. Serves 8.

NUTRITION INFORMATION 1 serving: 59 Calories; 2.2 g Total Fat (0.3 g Sat., 1.5 mg Cholesterol); 238 mg Sodium; 3 g Protein; 9 g Carbohydrate; 2 g Dietary Fiber

CHOICES 1 Fruit & Vegetable

Pictured on page 143.

To trim the coarse ends from asparagus spears, hold spear head in one hand and hold the stalk end in the other. Bend until stalk end snaps off. The spear will break where the tender part starts and the dry portion begins.

· S I D E   D I S H E S ·

Crumbed Broccoli

Serve immediately after combining with crumbs to prevent sogginess. Subtle garlic taste and interesting texture from the crumbs.

Olive oil	2 tsp.	10 mL
Finely chopped jalapeño pepper, ribs and seeds removed (see Tip, page 101)	1 tbsp.	15 mL
Dry whole wheat bread crumbs	$^1/_3$ cup	75 mL
Garlic cloves, minced	3	3
Olive oil	2 tsp.	10 mL
Water	$^1/_4$ cup	60 mL
Head of broccoli, stems thinly sliced and florets cut bite size	$1^1/_2$ lbs.	680 g

Heat first amount of olive oil in small non-stick frying pan on medium. Sauté hot pepper for 30 seconds to 1 minute until slightly soft. Add bread crumbs. Sauté until crumbs are toasted and golden brown. Set aside.

Sauté garlic in second amount of olive oil until sizzling but not brown. Add water. Bring to a boil. Add broccoli stems on bottom of frying pan and florets on top. Cover. Heat on low for 5 to 6 minutes until broccoli is bright green and tender-crisp. Drain. Toss broccoli with crumbs in medium bowl. Makes $3^1/_2$ cups (875 mL).

NUTRITION INFORMATION $^2/_3$ cup (150 mL): 86 Calories; 3.7 g Total Fat (0.5 g Sat., 0.1 mg Cholesterol); 78 mg Sodium; 4 g Protein; 11 g Carbohydrate; 3 g Dietary Fiber

CHOICES 1 Fruit & Vegetable; $^1/_2$ Fat & Oil

Roasted Veggies

Love that sweet roasted flavor. Make use of the many different salt-free herb preparations to change the flavor whenever you want!

Red baby potatoes (about 10), halved	1 lb.	454 g
Baby carrots (finger size), about 8 oz. (225 g)	$1^3/_4$ cups	425 mL
Large cauliflower florets (about 10 oz., 285 g)	$2^1/_4$ cups	550 mL
Parsnips, cut into 1 inch (2.5 cm) thick slices (about 8 oz., 225 g)	4	4
Olive oil	1 tbsp.	15 mL
Water	1 tbsp.	15 mL
Garlic clove, minced (optional)	1	1
No-salt Italian herb seasoning (such as Mrs. Dash)	1 tbsp.	15 mL
Salt	$^1/_2$ tsp.	2 mL
Freshly ground pepper, sprinkle		

Combine first 4 ingredients in lightly greased 9 x 13 inch (22 x 33 cm) pan.

(continued on next page)

Combine remaining 6 ingredients in small dish. Pour over vegetables. Toss well. Bake, covered, in 450°F (230°C) oven for 30 minutes. Stir. Bake, uncovered, for 30 minutes until vegetables are tender and starting to turn brown. Serves 4.

1 serving: 210 Calories; 4 g Total Fat (0.6 g Sat., 0 mg Cholesterol); 384 mg Sodium; 5 g Protein; 41 g Carbohydrate; 7 g Dietary Fiber

CHOICES 1¹/₂ Starch; 2 Fruit & Vegetable; ¹/₂ Fat & Oil

Stuffed Tomatoes

Fresh flavor with a hint of tangy feta.

Large tomatoes	6	6
Chopped onion	1 cup	250 mL
Garlic cloves, minced	2	2
Olive oil	2 tsp.	10 mL
Chopped fresh mushrooms	1 cup	250 mL
Diced zucchini, with peel	1¹/₂ cups	375 mL
Salt	¹/₂ tsp.	2 mL
Chopped fresh sweet basil (or 1 tsp., 5 mL, dried)	1 tbsp.	15 mL
Chopped fresh oregano leaves (or 1 tsp., 5 mL, dried)	1 tbsp.	15 mL
Whole wheat cracker crumbs	¹/₃ cup	75 mL
Crumbled feta cheese (about 4 oz., 113 g)	²/₃ cup	150 g
Margarine	2 tsp.	10 mL
Whole wheat cracker crumbs	¹/₄ cup	60 mL
Finely chopped fresh parsley (or 1 tsp., 5 mL, flakes)	1 tbsp.	15 mL

Cut ¹/₄ inch (6 mm) slice from stem end of tomatoes. Scoop out pulp. Chop pulp fine. Set aside. Turn hollowed tomatoes upside down on paper towels to drain.

Sauté onion and garlic in olive oil in large non-stick frying pan on medium-high until onion is soft. Stir in mushrooms and zucchini. Sauté until soft.

Stir in salt, basil, oregano and first amount of cracker crumbs. Add cheese. Add reserved tomato pulp. Stir. Makes 5¹/₄ cups (1.3 L) filling. Fill tomato cavities.

Melt margarine in small saucepan. Stir in second amount of cracker crumbs and parsley. Sprinkle about 2¹/₂ tsp. (12 mL) over each tomato. Place tomatoes in 9 x 13 inch (22 x 33 cm) baking pan. Pour in about ¹/₂ inch (12 mm) water. Bake, uncovered, in 350°F (175°C) oven for about 30 minutes until heated through. Makes 6 stuffed tomatoes.

1 stuffed tomato: 187 Calories; 10.3 g Total Fat (4.8 g Sat., 23 mg Cholesterol); 594 mg Sodium; 7 g Protein; 20 g Carbohydrate; 4 g Dietary Fiber

CHOICES ¹/₂ Starch; 1 Fruit & Vegetable; ¹/₂ Protein; 2 Fat & Oil

Pictured on page 72.

Caramelized Onion Strata

Good onion taste complements the tomatoes and crispy rye top.

Thinly sliced onion	2 cups	500 mL
Canola oil	1 tsp.	5 mL
Brown sugar, packed	1 tsp.	5 mL
Apple cider vinegar	1 tbsp.	15 mL
Rye bread cubes	6 cups	1.5 L
Medium roma (plum) tomatoes, seeded and diced	4	4
Salt	$1/2$ tsp.	2 mL
Freshly ground pepper, sprinkle		
Dried whole oregano	$1/2$ tsp.	2 mL
No-salt herb seasoning (such as Mrs. Dash)	1 tsp.	5 mL
Grated light Swiss cheese	$3/4$ cup	175 mL
Frozen egg product, thawed (see Note)	1 cup	250 mL
Skim evaporated milk	$3/4$ cup	175 mL
Skim milk	$3/4$ cup	175 mL
Dry mustard	$1/2$ tsp.	2 mL
Grated light Swiss cheese	$3/4$ cup	175 mL

Sauté onion in canola oil on medium in large non-stick frying pan for about 5 minutes until softened. Stir in brown sugar and vinegar. Sauté for 4 to 5 minutes until deep golden.

Arrange $1/2$ of bread cubes in greased 3 quart (3 L) shallow casserole. Layer onion mixture, tomato, salt, pepper, herb seasoning and oregano. Sprinkle with first amount of cheese. Top with remaining bread cubes.

Beat egg product, both milks and mustard in medium bowl. Pour evenly over bread cubes. Cover. Chill for several hours or overnight.

Bake, uncovered, in 325°F (160°C) oven for 1 hour. Sprinkle with second amount of cheese. Bake for about 15 minutes until set in center. Serves 6.

NUTRITION INFORMATION 1 serving: 268 Calories; 6.5 g Total Fat (0.2 g Sat., 1.8 mg Cholesterol); 613 mg Sodium; 22 g Protein; 33 g Carbohydrate; 3 g Dietary Fiber

CHOICES 1 Starch; 1 Fruit & Vegetable; 1 Milk; 2 Protein

Note: 4 tbsp. (50 mL) =1 large egg

One slice of bread will make about $3/4$ cup (175 mL) fresh bread crumbs or about $1/4$ cup (60 mL) fine dry bread crumbs.

Soups

ℕothing beats a bowl of nourishing, hot soup on a chilly day, so we've compiled a collection of delicious concoctions to warm you up. Pull up to the table with a bun or sandwich alongside your soup for an easy and satisfying meal.

Lentil Soup

This thick, hearty soup is a meal in itself. Serve with crusty bread or buns.

Lean ground chicken	**8 oz.**	**225 g**
Chopped onion	**$^1/_2$ cup**	**125 mL**
Sliced fresh mushrooms	**1 cup**	**250 mL**
Canola oil	**2 tsp.**	**10 mL**
Water	**5 cups**	**1.25 L**
Can of diced tomatoes, with juice	**28 oz.**	**796 mL**
Chopped cabbage	**2 cups**	**500 mL**
Sliced celery	**1 cup**	**250 mL**
Diced carrot	**1 cup**	**250 mL**
Diced green (or other) pepper	**$^1/_2$ cup**	**125 mL**
Bay leaves	**2**	**2**
Vegetable bouillon powder	**2 tsp.**	**10 mL**
Worcestershire sauce	**$^1/_2$ tsp.**	**2 mL**
Dried thyme leaves	**$^1/_2$ tsp.**	**2 mL**
Green lentils	**$^3/_4$ cup**	**175 mL**

Sauté chicken, onion and mushrooms in canola oil in large uncovered pot or Dutch oven until starting to brown. Drain.

Add remaining 11 ingredients to chicken. Bring to a boil. Reduce heat. Partially cover. Simmer for 45 minutes until lentils and vegetables are tender. Makes 10 cups (2.5 L).

NUTRITION INFORMATION 1 cup (250 mL): 120 Calories; 1.7 g Total Fat (0.2 g Sat., 13.1 mg Cholesterol); 288 mg Sodium; 11 g Protein; 16 g Carbohydrate; 4 g Dietary Fiber

CHOICES $^1/_2$ Starch; 1 Fruit & Vegetable; 1 Protein

Pictured on page 144.

Barley Vegetable Soup

Thick, hearty soup warms the insides on a cold winter day.

Water	2 qts.	2 L
Pearl barley	1 cup	250 mL
Chopped onion	1 cup	250 mL
Chopped celery	1 cup	250 mL
Diced carrot	1 cup	250 mL
Vegetable bouillon powder	2 tbsp.	30 mL
Medium potatoes, peeled and diced	2	2
Worcestershire sauce	1 1/2 tsp.	7 mL
Dried sweet basil	1 1/2 tsp.	7 mL
Parsley flakes	1 tsp.	5 mL
Freshly ground pepper, sprinkle		
Vegetable cocktail juice	1 cup	250 mL
All-purpose flour	2 tbsp.	30 mL

Put first 6 ingredients into large uncovered pot or Dutch oven. Cover. Simmer for 30 minutes.

Add next 5 ingredients. Cover. Simmer for 15 minutes until potato is tender.

Whisk vegetable juice and flour in small bowl until smooth. Stir into soup. Simmer for 1 minute until slightly thickened. Makes 10 1/2 cups (2.6 L).

NUTRITION INFORMATION 1 cup (250 mL): 117 Calories; 0.6 g Total Fat (0.2 g Sat., 0.2 mg Cholesterol); 456 mg Sodium; 4 g Protein; 26 g Carbohydrate; 4 g Dietary Fiber

CHOICES 1 Starch; 1 Fruit & Vegetable

1. Barley And Rice Pilaf, page 134
2. Italian Potato Casserole, page 129
3. Cold Dressed Asparagus, page 137

Minestrone Soup

Thick and chunky with a rich-tasting broth. A hearty meal with some bread or buns.

Container of Tomato Vegetable Sauce (3 cups, 750 mL), page 106, thawed	1	1
Water	4 cups	1 L
Sliced celery rib	1/2 cup	125 mL
Finely diced carrot	1/2 cup	125 mL
Chopped cabbage	1 cup	250 mL
Beef bouillon powder	2 tsp.	10 mL
Granulated sugar	1 tsp.	5 mL
No-salt garlic and herb seasoning (such as Mrs. Dash)	1 tsp.	5 mL
Dried crushed chilies	1/8 tsp.	0.5 mL
Can of kidney beans, drained	14 oz.	398 mL
Whole wheat elbow macaroni	1/2 cup	125 mL

Grated Parmesan cheese (optional)

Combine sauce and water in large saucepan. Bring to a boil. Add next 7 ingredients. Cover. Simmer for 30 minutes.

Stir in kidney beans and macaroni. Cover. Bring to a boil. Cook for 10 minutes, stirring twice, until pasta is tender.

Sprinkle individual servings with Parmesan cheese. Makes 7 cups (1.75 L).

NUTRITION INFORMATION 1 cup (250 mL): 120 Calories; 1.3 g Total Fat (0.2 g Sat., 0.1 mg Cholesterol); 406 mg Sodium; 6 g Protein; 24 g Carbohydrate; 6 g Dietary Fiber

CHOICES 1 Starch; 1 Fruit & Vegetable; 1/2 Protein

1. Lentil Soup, page 141
2. White Bean Soup, page 146
3. Curried Zucchini Chowder, page 148

• SOUPS •

White Bean Soup

The list of ingredients might seem lengthy, but you can be eating hot soup in an hour from start to finish.

Sliced leeks (halved lengthwise and rinsed well)	1 cup	250 mL
Chopped celery heart and leaves	1 cup	250 mL
Garlic cloves, minced	2	2
Olive oil	2 tsp.	10 mL
Diced carrot	1 cup	250 mL
Diced potato	1 cup	250 mL
Can of Italian spiced tomatoes, with juice, puréed	14 oz.	398 mL
Water	4 cups	1 L
Chicken bouillon powder	1 tbsp.	15 mL
Hot pepper sauce	$\frac{1}{2}$ tsp.	2 mL
Celery seed	$\frac{1}{2}$ tsp.	2 mL
Salt	$\frac{1}{2}$ tsp.	2 mL
Freshly ground pepper	$\frac{1}{8}$ tsp.	0.5 mL
Dried sweet basil (optional)	$\frac{1}{2}$ tsp.	2 mL
Fennel seed, crushed (optional)	$\frac{1}{4}$ tsp.	1 mL
Can of white kidney beans, drained and rinsed	19 oz.	540 mL
Shredded fresh spinach leaves, packed	1 cup	250 mL
Finely chopped fresh parsley (or 1 tsp., 5 mL, flakes)	1 tbsp.	15 mL

Sauté leeks, celery and garlic in olive oil in large uncovered pot or Dutch oven until softened.

Add next 9 ingredients. Bring to a boil. Reduce heat. Simmer, partially covered, for 10 to 15 minutes until carrot and potato are tender.

Stir in remaining 5 ingredients. Cover. Simmer for 5 minutes until spinach is softened. Makes 8 cups (2 L).

NUTRITION INFORMATION 1 cup (250 mL): 104 Calories; 1.7 g Total Fat (0.3 g Sat., 0.2 mg Cholesterol); 655 mg Sodium; 5 g Protein; 19 g Carbohydrate; 2 g Dietary Fiber

CHOICES 1 Starch; $\frac{1}{2}$ Fruit & Vegetable; $\frac{1}{2}$ Protein

Pictured on page 144 and on back cover.

A mild onion, such as Spanish or Walla Walla varieties, can be substituted for leeks in a recipe.

Roasted Garlic Soup

Roast some garlic the next time you have your oven on to make this special soup. Serve small amounts for an elegant first course.

Large heads of garlic (not individual cloves)	4	4
Olive oil	2 tsp.	10 mL
Water	1/4 cup	60 mL
Chopped onion	2/3 cup	150 mL
Olive oil	2 tsp.	10 mL
Peeled and diced potato	3 cups	750 mL
Can of condensed chicken broth	10 oz.	284 mL
Water	2/3 cup	150 mL
Dried tarragon	1 tsp.	5 mL
Granulated sugar	1 tsp.	5 mL
Salt	1/2 tsp.	2 mL
Cayenne pepper	1/8 tsp.	0.5 mL
Can of skim evaporated milk	13 1/2 oz.	385 mL
All-purpose flour	2 tbsp.	30 mL
White (or alcohol-free) wine	1/2 cup	125 mL

Remove loose papery skin from garlic heads, being careful not separate or peel individual cloves. Cut tops off garlic heads to barely expose tops of some cloves. Place in garlic baker or small pie plate. Drizzle 1/2 tsp. (2 mL) of first amount of olive oil over each garlic head. Drizzle water into baking dish. Cover tightly with lid or foil. Bake in 350°F (175°C) oven for about 45 minutes until garlic cloves are soft and golden. Cool enough to handle. Squeeze out cloves into small bowl.

Sauté onion in second amount of olive oil in large saucepan until soft. Add potato, broth and water. Cover. Simmer for about 15 minutes until potato is very tender.

Stir in roasted garlic. Add tarragon, sugar, salt and cayenne. Purée in blender or food processor until smooth. Return to saucepan. Bring to a boil.

Stir evaporated milk into flour in small bowl until smooth. Add to soup. Heat and stir on medium until slightly thickened. Add wine. Stir. Makes 6 cups (1.5 L).

NUTRITION INFORMATION 1 cup (250 mL): 238 Calories; 4 g Total Fat (0.7 g Sat., 3 mg Cholesterol); 632 mg Sodium; 12 g Protein; 37 g Carbohydrate; 2 g Dietary Fiber
CHOICES 1 Starch; 1 Fruit & Vegetable; 1 1/2 Milk; 1/2 Protein; 1/2 Fat & Oil

To keep garlic bulbs from sprouting, softening and drying out, store in a container in the freezer. To easily peel a clove at a time, heat on high (100%) for 30 seconds in microwave.

Chilled Vegetable Soup

A refreshing soup that uses up those bits of fresh herbs and vegetables in the refrigerator!

Vegetable cocktail juice	2¹/₂ cups	625 mL
Diced fresh tomato	2 cups	500 mL
Water	1 cup	250 mL
Diced red or green sweet pepper	1 cup	250 mL
Diced cucumber, with peel	1 cup	250 mL
Chopped green onion	¹/₂ cup	125 mL
Chopped fresh chives (or 1 tsp., 5 mL, dried)	1 tbsp.	15 mL
Chopped fresh oregano leaves (or ¹/₂ tsp., 2 mL, dried)	1 tbsp.	15 mL
Chopped fresh sweet basil (or 2 tsp., 10 mL, dried)	2 tbsp.	30 mL
Lemon juice	2 tbsp.	30 mL
Light sour cream, for garnish		
Hot pepper sauce, for garnish		

Combine first 10 ingredients in large bowl. Chill for several hours or overnight.

Purée ¹/₂ in blender or food processor. Return to bowl. Stir. Spoon into individual serving bowls. Add dollop of sour cream and dash of pepper sauce if desired. Makes 7³/₄ cups (1.9 L).

NUTRITION INFORMATION 1 cup (250 mL): 34 Calories; 0.3 g Total Fat (trace Sat., 0 mg Cholesterol); 306 mg Sodium; 1 g Protein; 8 g Carbohydrate; 1 g Dietary Fiber

CHOICES 1 Fruit & Vegetable

Curried Zucchini Chowder

The curry flavor is mild but a swirl of yogurt, sour cream or cream in the soup at serving time will mellow the flavor even more.

Chopped onion	1 cup	250 mL
Garlic clove, minced	1	1
Margarine	2 tsp.	10 mL
Curry paste (available in Asian section of grocery store)	¹/₂ tsp.	2 mL
Grated zucchini (about 3 medium), with peel	4 cups	1 L
Diced potato	3 cups	750 mL
Water	3¹/₄ cups	800 mL
Vegetable bouillon powder	2 tbsp.	30 mL
Bay leaf	1	1
Freshly ground pepper	¹/₄ tsp.	1 mL
Ground cumin	¹/₁₆ tsp.	0.5 mL

(continued on next page)

Sauté onion and garlic in margarine in large uncovered pot or Dutch oven until onion is very soft and turning golden brown. Stir in curry paste. Sauté for 1 minute.

Stir in remaining 7 ingredients. Heat on medium, partially covered, for 1 hour. Remove and discard bay leaf. Remove and reserve 2 cups (500 mL) soup. Process remaining soup with hand blender or in batches in blender until smooth. Combine reserved and puréed chowder. Makes 7 cups (1.75 L).

NUTRITION INFORMATION 1 cup (250 mL): 92 Calories; 1.6 g Total Fat (0.4 g Sat., 0.3 mg Cholesterol); 530 mg Sodium; 3 g Protein; 18 g Carbohydrate; 3 g Dietary Fiber

CHOICES 1 Starch, $^1/_2$ Fruit & Vegetable

Pictured on page 144.

Bean And Bacon Soup

Rich, warm flavor from bacon. Hearty comfort food.

Chopped onion	$^2/_3$ cup	150 mL
Chopped celery	$^2/_3$ cup	150 mL
Garlic cloves, minced	2	2
Canola oil	2 tsp.	10 mL
Canadian back bacon, diced	2 oz.	57 g
Water	5 cups	1.25 L
Vegetable bouillon powder	1 tbsp.	15 mL
Sliced carrot	1 cup	250 mL
Peeled, diced potato	2 cups	500 mL
Bay leaves	2	2
Can of mixed beans, drained and rinsed	19 oz.	540 mL
Can of baked beans in tomato sauce	14 oz.	398 mL

Sauté onion, celery and garlic in canola oil in large uncovered pot or Dutch oven until very soft. Add bacon. Sauté until starting to brown.

Add next 5 ingredients. Bring to a boil. Cover. Simmer for 25 minutes until potato is very tender and breaking up.

Stir in both beans. Heat, uncovered, for about 10 minutes until soup is thickened. Remove and discard bay leaves. Makes 8 cups (2 L).

NUTRITION INFORMATION 1 cup (250 mL): 160 Calories; 2.4 g Total Fat (0.4 g Sat., 3.7 mg Cholesterol); 626 mg Sodium; 8 g Protein; 29 g Carbohydrate; 8 g Dietary Fiber

CHOICES 2 Starch; 1 Protein

If your homemade soup is too salty, drop a raw potato into the pot and remove just before serving.

Turtle Bean Soup

Gentle heat from the chili powder and the hot pepper sauce.

Chopped onion	1 cup	250 mL
Canola oil	2 tsp.	10 mL
Garlic cloves, minced	2	2
Medium red pepper, diced	1	1
Water	4 cups	1 L
Vegetable bouillon powder	2 tbsp.	30 mL
Can of black beans, drained and rinsed	19 oz.	540 mL
Chili powder	1 1/2 tsp.	7 mL
Bay leaf	1	1
Dried whole marjoram (or oregano), crushed	1/2 tsp.	2 mL
Dried sweet basil	1 tsp.	5 mL
Kernel corn, fresh or frozen	1/2 cup	125 mL
Lime juice	2 tsp.	10 mL
Hot pepper sauce	1/2 tsp.	2 mL
Cooked, mashed (or 1 cup, 250 mL, grated raw) potato	1 cup	250 mL
Chopped fresh parsley	1/4 cup	60 mL
Chopped fresh cilantro (optional)	1 tbsp.	15 mL
Non-fat plain yogurt (or low-fat sour cream), optional		
Sliced green onion (optional)		

Sauté onion in canola oil in large uncovered pot or Dutch oven until soft. Add garlic and red pepper. Sauté for about 2 minutes until pepper is soft.

Stir in next 11 ingredients. Cover. Simmer on medium-low for 40 minutes.

Remove and discard bay leaf. Stir in parsley and cilantro. See Tip, below. Spoon into individual serving bowls. Top with a dollop of yogurt and sprinkle of green onion. Makes 6 cups (1.5 L).

NUTRITION INFORMATION 1 cup (250 mL): 148 Calories; 2.5 g Total Fat (0.4 g Sat., 0.4 mg Cholesterol); 711 mg Sodium; 6 g Protein; 27 g Carbohydrate; 4 g Dietary Fiber

CHOICES 1 1/2 Starch; 1/2 Fruit & Vegetable; 1/2 Protein

Variation: To make a thicker soup, purée 3 cups (750 mL) soup in blender. Return to pot. Heat through.

Measurement Tables

Throughout this book measurements are given in Conventional and Metric measure. To compensate for differences between the two measurements due to rounding, a full metric measure is not always used. The cup used is the standard 8 fluid ounce. Temperature is given in degrees Fahrenheit and Celsius. Baking pan measurements are in inches and centimetres as well as quarts and litres. An exact metric conversion is given below as well as the working equivalent (Standard Measure).

OVEN TEMPERATURES

Fahrenheit (°F)	Celsius (°C)
175°	80°
200°	95°
225°	110°
250°	120°
275°	140°
300°	150°
325°	160°
350°	175°
375°	190°
400°	205°
425°	220°
450°	230°
475°	240°
500°	260°

PANS

Conventional Inches	Metric Centimetres
8x8 inch	20x20 cm
9x9 inch	22x22 cm
9x13 inch	22x33 cm
10x15 inch	25x38 cm
11x17 inch	28x43 cm
8x2 inch round	20x5 cm
9x2 inch round	22x5 cm
10x4¹/₂ inch tube	25x11 cm
8x4x3 inch loaf	20x10x7.5 cm
9x5x3 inch loaf	22x12.5x7.5 cm

SPOONS

Conventional Measure	Metric Exact Conversion Millilitre (mL)	Metric Standard Measure Millilitre (mL)
¹/₈ teaspoon (tsp.)	0.6 mL	0.5 mL
¹/₄ teaspoon (tsp.)	1.2 mL	1 mL
¹/₂ teaspoon (tsp.)	2.4 mL	2 mL
1 teaspoon (tsp.)	4.7 mL	5 mL
2 teaspoons (tsp.)	9.4 mL	10 mL
1 tablespoon (tbsp.)	14.2 mL	15 mL

CUPS

¹/₄ cup (4 tbsp.)	56.8 mL	60 mL
¹/₃ cup (5¹/₃ tbsp.)	75.6 mL	75 mL
¹/₂ cup (8 tbsp.)	113.7 mL	125 mL
²/₃ cup (10²/₃ tbsp.)	151.2 mL	150 mL
³/₄ cup (12 tbsp.)	170.5 mL	175 mL
1 cup (16 tbsp.)	227.3 mL	250 mL
4¹/₂ cups	1022.9 mL	1000 mL (1 L)

DRY MEASUREMENTS

Conventional Measure Ounces (oz.)	Metric Exact Conversion Grams (g)	Metric Standard Measure Grams (g)
1 oz.	28.3 g	28 g
2 oz.	56.7 g	57 g
3 oz.	85.0 g	85 g
4 oz.	113.4 g	125 g
5 oz.	141.7 g	140 g
6 oz.	170.1 g	170 g
7 oz.	198.4 g	200 g
8 oz.	226.8 g	250 g
16 oz.	453.6 g	500 g
32 oz.	907.2 g	1000 g (1 kg)

CASSEROLES (Canada & Britain)

Standard Size Casserole	Exact Metric Measure
1 qt. (5 cups)	1.13 L
1¹/₂ qts. (7¹/₂ cups)	1.69 L
2 qts. (10 cups)	2.25 L
2¹/₂ qts. (12¹/₂ cups)	2.81 L
3 qts. (15 cups)	3.38 L
4 qts. (20 cups)	4.5 L
5 qts. (25 cups)	5.63 L

CASSEROLES (United States)

Standard Size Casserole	Exact Metric Measure
1 qt. (4 cups)	900 mL
1¹/₂ qts. (6 cups)	1.35 L
2 qts. (8 cups)	1.8 L
2¹/₂ qts. (10 cups)	2.25 L
3 qts. (12 cups)	2.7 L
4 qts. (16 cups)	3.6 L
5 qts. (20 cups)	4.5 L

Index

Photo Index

Tip Index

Company's Coming cookbooks are available at **retail locations** throughout Canada!

See mail order form

Buy any 2 cookbooks—choose a 3rd FREE of equal or less value than the lowest price paid.   *Available in French

Original Series	CA$14.99 Canada	US$10.99 USA & International

CODE		CODE		CODE	
SQ	150 Delicious Squares*	DE	Desserts	PA	Pasta*
AP	Appetizers	KC	Kids Cooking*	PI	Pies*
AC	Appliance Cooking*	LCA	Light Casseroles*	PZ	Pizza!*
	NEW (April 1/01)	LR	Light Recipes*	PR	Preserves*
BA	Barbecues*	LFC	Low-Fat Cooking*	SA	Salads*
BR	Breads*	LFP	Low-Fat Pasta*	SC	Slow Cooker Recipes*
BB	Breakfasts & Brunches*	MC	Main Courses	SS	Soups & Sandwiches
CK	Cakes	MAM	Make-Ahead Meals*	ST	Starters*
CA	Casseroles*	ME	Meatless Cooking*	SF	Stir-Fry*
CH	Chicken, Etc.*	MI	Microwave Cooking*	PB	The Potato Book*
CO	Cookies*	MU	Muffins & More*	VE	Vegetables
CT	Cooking For Two*	ODM	One-Dish Meals*		

Greatest Hits	CA$12.99 Canada	US$9.99 USA & International

CODE		CODE		CODE	
BML	Biscuits, Muffins & Loaves*	MEX	Mexican* **NEW** (May 1/01)	SAW	Sandwiches & Wraps
DSD	Dips, Spreads & Dressings*	ITAL	Italian* **NEW** (May 1/01)	SAS	Soups & Salads

Lifestyle Series	CA$16.99 Canada	US$12.99 USA & International

CODE		CODE	
GR	Grilling*	LFP	Low-fat Pasta*
LFC	Low-fat Cooking*	DC	Diabetic Cooking* **NEW**

Special Occasion Series	CA$19.99 Canada	US$19.99 USA & International

CODE	
CE	Chocolate Everything*

www.**companys**coming.com
visit our web-site

COMPANY'S COMING PUBLISHING LIMITED
2311 - 96 Street
Edmonton, Alberta, Canada T6N 1G3
Tel: (780) 450-6223 Fax: (780) 450-1857

Mail Order Form

See reverse for list of cookbooks

QUANTITY	CODE	TITLE	PRICE EACH	PRICE TOTAL
			$	$

DON'T FORGET to indicate your FREE book(s). (see exclusive mail order offer above) PLEASE PRINT

TOTAL BOOKS (including FREE)

TOTAL BOOKS PURCHASED: $

	INTERNATIONAL	CANADA & USA
Plus Shipping & Handling (PER DESTINATION)	$ 7.00 (one book)	$ 5.00 (1-3 books)
Additional Books (INCLUDING FREE BOOKS)	$ ($2.00 each)	$ ($1.00 each)
SUB-TOTAL	$	$
Canadian residents add G.S.T(7%)		$
TOTAL AMOUNT ENCLOSED	$	$

The Fine Print

- Orders outside Canada must be **PAID IN US FUNDS** by cheque or money order drawn on Canadian or US bank or by credit card.
- Make cheque or money order payable to: **COMPANY'S COMING PUBLISHING LIMITED.**
- Prices are expressed in Canadian dollars for Canada, US dollars for USA & International and are subject to change without prior notice.
- Orders are shipped surface mail. For courier rates, visit our web-site: **www.companyscoming.com** or contact us: **Tel: (780) 450-6223 Fax: (780) 450-1857.**
- Sorry, no C.O.D's.

☐ MasterCard ☐ VISA

_____ Expiry date

Account # _____

Name of cardholder _____

Cardholder's signature _____

Shipping Address

Send the cookbooks listed above to:

Name: _____

Street: _____

City: _____ Prov./State: _____

Country: _____ Postal Code/Zip: _____

Tel: ( ) _____

E-mail address: _____

Gift Giving

- Let us help you with your gift giving!
- We will send cookbooks directly to the recipients of your choice if you give us their names and addresses.
- Please specify the titles you wish to send to each person.
- If you would like to include your personal note or card, we will be pleased to enclose it with your gift order.
- Company's Coming Cookbooks make excellent gifts: Birthdays, bridal showers, Mother's Day, Father's Day, graduation or any occasion... collect them all!

Please mail or fax to:
Company's Coming Publishing Limited
2311 - 96 Street
Edmonton, Alberta, Canada   T6N 1G3
Fax: (780) 450-1857

Name: _____
Address: _____
_____
e-mail: _____

Reader Survey

**We welcome your comments and would love to hear from you.
Please take a few moments to give us your feedback.**

1. *Approximately what percentage of the cooking do you do in your home?* _____ %

2. *How many meals do you cook in your home in a typical week?* _____

3. *How often do you refer to a cookbook (or other source) for recipes?*

   ❑ Everyday   ❑ 2 or 3 times a month   ❑ A few times a year
   ❑ A few times a week   ❑ Once a month   ❑ Never

4. *What recipe features are most important to you? Rank 1 to 7;
   (1 being most important, 7 being least important).*

   _____ Recipes for everyday cooking
   _____ Recipes for guests and entertaining
   _____ Easy recipes; quick to prepare, with everyday ingredients
   _____ Low-fat or health-conscious recipes
   _____ Recipes you can trust to work
   _____ Recipes using exotic ingredients
   _____ Recipes using fresh ingredients only

5. *What cookbook features are most important to you? Rank 1 to 6;
   (1 being most important, 6 being least important).*

   _____ Lots of color photographs of recipes
   _____ "How-to" instructions or photos
   _____ Helpful hints & cooking tips
   _____ Lay-flat binding (coil or plastic comb)
   _____ Well organized with complete index
   _____ Priced low

6. *How many cookbooks have you purchased in the last 12 months?*

7. *Of these, how many were gifts?* _____

8. *Age group*

   ❑ Under 18   ❑ 25 to 34   ❑ 45 to 54   ❑ 65+
   ❑ 18 to 24   ❑ 35 to 44   ❑ 55 to 64

9. *What do you like best about Company's Coming Cookbooks?*

   _____
   _____

10. *How could Company's Coming Cookbooks be improved?*

    _____
    _____

11. *What topics would you like to see published by Company's Coming?*

    _____
    _____

Thank you for sharing your views. We truly value your input.

DC1